WINNING THE FIGHT

A CONCEPTUAL FRAMEWORK FOR
COMBAT PERFORMANCE ENHANCEMENT

Special Tactics, LLC

Special Tactics and the Special Tactics Logo are registered trademarks of Special Tactics, LLC

© 2017 by Special Tactics, LLC

ISBN 978-1-945137-11-2

Except as permitted under U.S. Copyright Law, no part of this book may be reprinted, reproduced, transmitted, or utilized in any form by any electronic, mechanical, or other means, now known or hereafter invented, including photocopying, microfilming, and recording, or in any information storage or retrieval system, without written permission from Special Tactics, LLC.

Table of Contents

Introduction 1

    The Problem: Preparing for the Unexpected   2

    The First Priority: Repairing Organizational Dysfunction   4

    The Cause of Organizational Dysfunction: Blindness   5

A Framework for Combat Performance Enhancement 7

    Step 1: Recognize the Presence of Dysfunction   7

        Mistakes vs. Dysfunction   8

        Controllable vs. Uncontrollable   8

        Searching for Dysfunction with the Spot Check Method   10

        The Error of Viewing Dysfunction as Empirical Law   11

    Step 2: Diagnose the Dysfunction   13

        Functional Model for the Military Machine   17

        Diagnosing Dysfunction Along a Causal Chain   29

        The Importance of Considering Multiple Influences   30

        Which Cause Is Most Critical, Which Is Most Changeable?   31

    Step 3: Prescribe Specific Actions to Repair Dysfunction   32

        Identifying Leverage Points in the Context of Time Constraints   34

        Developing Pattern Recognition through Training and Wargaming   38

        Developing Pattern Recognition with Historical Case Studies   40

        Measuring Results   43

    Step 4: Anticipate Obstacles and Develop Counters   46

    Summary: From Concept to Application   47

Application of the Functional Model 51

Strategy 55

    The Nine Elements of Strategy   56
        Theory of Victory   56
        Prioritized Threats or Goals   60
        Resource Allocation   62
        Comparative Capabilities Forecast   65
        Strengths and Weaknesses   67
        Constraints   71
        Enemy Perspective   72
        Contingencies   73
        Outcomes   75
    Training Strategists: Strategic Science vs. Strategic Genius   76

Defense 79

    Defense Fundamentals   80
        Strategic and Operational Threat Assessment   80
        Enemy Courses of Action and Contingency Planning   81
    Cyclical Interplay between Operations and Intelligence   84
    Intelligence Planning and Indicators   87
        Planning for the Reserve   88
        Indicators and Alert Levels   89
    Wargaming and Backward Planning   91
    Counterattack   93

Intelligence 95

    Interaction of Intelligence and Operations   96
    The Intelligence Cycle   96
    Mechanics of the Intelligence System   98
        Requirements List   98
        Common Operating Picture   101
        Intelligence Products and Reports   102
    The Battle for Intelligence   104
        Denial, Deception and Offensive Counterintelligence   105
        Reconnaissance and the Fight for Intelligence on the Battlefield   107
    The Art of Intelligence and Common Pitfalls   110

Planning.. 113

Planning Timeline and Backward Planning	113
Subordinate Unit Initiative in the Planning Process	116
Flattening the Orders Process	118
Collaborative Planning	120
Risk Assessment, Course of Action Development and Contingencies	121
Briefings and Written Orders	126

Offense 129

Objectives in the Offense	129
Breaking the Enemy's Will	130
Deterrence	131
Political De-legitimization	132
Direct Attack on the Population	132
Annihilation of the Enemy Force	134
Capturing and Holding Key Terrain	135
Attriting the Enemy Force	137
Operational Shock	138
Strangulation	139
Regime Change	140
Multiple Objectives	141
Operational Methods	142
Combined Arms	143
Maneuver Warfare vs. Synchronization Warfare	144
Targeting	146
Initiative in the Offense	148
Simultaneity	149
Local Superiority and Defeat in Detail	150
Mobility in Offensive Operations	151
Assembling for Attack	151
Mobility and March Order	152
Deployment into Assault Formation	153
Fighting for the Objective and Sustaining the Advance	155

Training and Selection 157

- The Four Pillars of Effective Training — 158
  - Proper Mindset — 158
  - Situational Awareness — 159
  - Skill Proficiency — 160
  - Physical Fitness — 161
- Mastering the Basics — 162
  - Noel Burch's Four Stages of Learning — 163
  - Spontaneous Creative Action vs. Conditioned Response — 164
  - Repetitive Drill — 165
- Variable Patterns — 167
- Competitive Scenarios — 169
- Multimedia Sequencing — 171
- Prioritization and Tracking — 176
- Common Indicators of Poor Training — 178
- Selection — 182

To those who have gone before us, the living and the fallen

Introduction

Our purpose in writing this book is to help you, the reader, increase your chances of success in a real-world conflict. Thus, the analysis in this book is often more simplified and streamlined than that of most other academic works on military history and theory. In general, academic books aim to examine a specific question in detail to provide new intellectual insights. This book takes a wider view, seeking to understand war and conflict as a whole, in order to identify universal principles and patterns that might prove useful in real-world combat.

Given this practical focus, the following analysis and use of historical case studies does not aim to provide any definitive answers in the traditional, academic sense. Historical examples in this book may neglect the most important questions relating to a campaign and instead focus on minor details to illustrate more general concepts and recurring patterns in conflict.

In addition, this book does not seek to identify a single theory or model to explain human behavior or historical events. Strict adherence to a single theory or model is rarely helpful to the practitioner. Therefore, we encourage the reader to explore other books with different and even contradictory perspectives to those found in the following pages. The goal of this book is not to provide answers, but rather to stimulate thinking, improve performance and increase the chances of success on the battlefield.

We also ask the reader not to focus too much on the terms used in this book. In some cases, terms might be doctrinally correct but in other cases, the book may use outdated or non-doctrinal terms to explain concepts. Since military terms change constantly and different services and countries use different terms, it is counterproductive to place too much emphasis on the selection of terms. In most cases, the terms in this book were chosen because they provide the most descriptive and easily understandable expression of a concept.

We are also aware that this book is by necessity an incomplete discussion of modern warfare. The book leaves out many critical subjects and leaves many questions unanswered. Providing a comprehensive account of all aspects of warfare in a single volume is not only impossible, but an attempt to do so would likely prove unreadable or excessively long. By not attempting to cover everything, this book aims to be shorter, clearer and more useful to practitioners.

This book uses conventional warfare, primarily ground combat, as the medium for illuminating universal concepts that apply to all forms of conflict and combat. While the book may appear to be written only for military commanders, the concepts can prove useful in a wide variety of contexts including law enforcement, high-threat protection, and home defense. This book is also designed to be helpful to practitioners at all levels, from the newest recruit to the strategic decision maker. Providing this holistic view of conflict will encourage a common understanding and increase synergy between various levels of command.

The Problem: Preparing for the Unexpected

The uncertainty of war makes it very difficult for military professionals to know how to prepare themselves and improve performance across the force. The criticism that armies are tragically always prepared to "fight the last war" appears and reappears countless times throughout history. While that criticism may be valid, what is the alternative? Given that an army's only tangible experience and frame of reference comes from the last war, how is it possible to prepare for the next war when there is no way of knowing what the next war will look like? This problem not only applies to strategic thinkers planning for the next war, but also relates to the squad leader planning for the next patrol. Arguably the most challenging problem in warfare is how to prepare for the unexpected.

Attempting to anticipate possible contingencies is critical; however, even the most carefully analyzed predictions can prove to be misguided or catastrophically counterproductive. The better way to prepare for the unexpected is not to anticipate the problem but rather to focus on neutralizing all of the other controllable variables, in order to free up maximum bandwidth to confront the unexpected when it occurs.

While many variables in war are out of control, practitioners can control their own decisions and actions. Consider two military forces labeled A and B. Force A focuses on predicting future problems at the expense of improving basic performance, skills and capabilities. Force B still keeps potential problems in mind but rather immediately focuses on improving performance, in the quickest, simplest and most universally relevant ways, concentrating on fungible capabilities that will prove useful in any situation. Force B will rapidly pull ahead of Force A in effectiveness and probability of success.

In short, the best way to prepare for the unexpected is to focus on the basics. This is the core thesis of this book, which will reappear again and again in subsequent examinations of various elements of warfare.

The First Priority: Repairing Organizational Dysfunction

While the concept of focusing on the basics provides a general foundation for preparing for the unexpected and enhancing performance in an uncertain environment, there is an additional concept that can help make training and preparations more relevant and productive. Studying historical trends makes it clear that mission failure is less often the result of inadequate performance and more often the result of outright failure to perform as a result of organizational dysfunction. Essentially, forces generally do not fail because they are not good enough, but rather because some part of their unit or organization is simply broken, resulting in an inexcusable blunder that could have been easily avoided, had all systems been functioning properly.

Given this premise, when focusing on the basics, the first priority is ensuring the organizational "machine" itself is working properly. This calls for developing and exercising systems and testing them to ensure they are functional. This helps prevent foolish, avoidable mistakes. For example, a unit may spend 100 hours of training improving its average marksmanship accuracy by 10 percent. However, that unit might fail their next mission because they spent all their time shooting and failed to check if the batteries in their radios were fully charged. In terms of overall impact on the chances for mission success, the unit would have achieved better results by taking just a few hours to establish simple and functional procedures for charging batteries, and to conduct pre-combat checks prior to each mission.

This focus on systems may seem to contradict modern military philosophies that aim to nurture adaptability and creativity through decentralized command and control structures. Nothing could be further from the case. Forces that begin by focusing on the mechanical task of developing systems to repair organizational dysfunction ultimately have more time to think and train creatively and are less distracted by preventable mishaps. The military machine itself must work, in order for efforts to nurture creativity and adaptability to have the desired effect. The best race car driver in the world can never win a race in a car with no tires or fuel. Therefore, the focus on systems is not an end in itself, but is rather a necessary precondition for further evolution.

The focus on repairing dysfunction is also critical because dysfunction is a more serious and widespread problem than most leaders realize. As difficult as it might be to believe, both historical and contemporary studies show that combat units are frequently dysfunctional in many critical areas. When dysfunctional units must perform in a high-stress situation and put their systems and training to the test, the result is almost invariably catastrophic failure. A reprise of the infamous "Task Force Smith" debacle in the Korean War is always a looming possibility.

It can be counterproductive to provide contemporary, real-world examples of organizational dysfunction since they inevitably provoke controversy. However, most modern military or security professionals will agree that many cases of organizational dysfunction exist today. In general terms, if a unit is overrun, it may not be because they had a poor defense plan but rather because they had no defense plan. Performance failures in the field may not be the result of inadequate training, but rather the result of no training in a critical area. Essentially, some modern military units have components or capabilities that are simply missing or broken, and leaders may fail to recognize these deficiencies until it is too late.

The Cause of Organizational Dysfunction: Blindness

How is it possible for intelligent leaders to fail to see critical points of dysfunction in their own organizations? The reason is that without the need to constantly apply training and exercise systems, it is difficult to identify points of dysfunction. Military organizations in a time of war find it easier to learn and improve because the audit of battle provides immediate feedback on effectiveness. High performance, functional units win. Dysfunctional units with poor performance almost always lose. Improving in the absence of such clear feedback demands a mindset of constant improvement and systems that encourage frequent, realistic and unbiased organizational self-assessment. Organizations that do not proactively self-assess can grow so accustomed to overlooking mediocrity that they fail to question their real capabilities and descend into a state of blindness to their own faults.

In many such organizations, looking the part or wearing the appropriate rank or shoulder patch often passes for professionalism, while real levels of competence or performance are unknown. When an organization's true level of performance is not known, the possibility of critical organizational dysfunction emerges. Leaders and units at all levels must be put to the test before it is possible to determine their real level of performance and whether they are functional or dysfunctional. This self-assessment process drives subsequent training and preparation efforts to enhance performance. The following section provides four practical steps for counteracting blindness and dysfunction in order to enhance performance in the fastest and most relevant ways.

A Framework for Combat Performance Enhancement

The four steps of performance enhancement are, 1) recognize the presence of dysfunction, 2) diagnose dysfunction, 3) prescribe actions to repair the dysfunction, 4) anticipate obstacles and develop counters. The following section examines each of these four steps in detail and explains how they lead to increased performance enhancement.

Step 1: Recognize the Presence of Dysfunction

As described, the main reason why dysfunction can exist and thrive in experienced organizations, under the noses of intelligent leaders, is due to a state of blindness resulting from lack of honest self-assessment. If responsible leaders knew that their organizations were dysfunctional, they would take steps to correct the dysfunction. Thus, the first and most critical step in performance enhancement is to recognize the presence of dysfunction in the first place. To recognize dysfunction, it is crucial to understand exactly what dysfunction is and how it differs from honest mistakes.

Mistakes vs. Dysfunction

Mistakes are often unavoidable and inherent to all human endeavors, while dysfunction highlights a deficiency, weakness, or lack of capability and implies that something is not working the way it is supposed to work. Dysfunction is less excusable than a mistake. Even the most skilled professionals can make an honest mistake. Dysfunction implies some sort of inexcusable deficiency. More importantly, dysfunction has a clear, definable opposite: function. The fact that something is not working implies that definable steps must exist to make it work properly.

Dysfunction most often takes the form of a piece of the "military machine" that is simply missing, or a unit that has entirely failed to prepare or practice for a predictable contingency. If an intelligence staff officer fails to report information accurately, that may be a mistake. If the reason for the reporting failure is a lack of established reporting procedures, the officer was never trained how to properly report or didn't practice on a regular basis, that mistake becomes a dysfunction.

If a squad panics when their truck is struck by a roadside bomb and some of its members die because the squad cannot figure out how to load and evacuate casualties fast enough, that might be a mistake. However, if the reason for the panic is that the squad did not have any pre-rehearsed drills for reacting to a roadside bomb and evacuating casualties, that is dysfunction. If the squad had a drill but never practiced it, that is also a dysfunction. Mistakes are often unavoidable; dysfunction is clearly solvable.

Controllable vs. Uncontrollable

The most important reason to target dysfunction as opposed to mistakes is because the problem of dysfunction can be solved, while mistakes are inevitable. This relates to the earlier discussion of preparing for the unexpected by controlling what is controllable. It is easier to control improvements in functionality and capability than it is to guarantee no mistakes in a hypothetical future scenario. This concept lies at the foundation of effective performance enhancement.

The concept of controlling the controllables applies at all levels of warfare. Experienced military professionals know that friction is inevitable in combat and that what can go wrong will go wrong. When a poorly trained unit encounters an unexpected problem, it can focus only 10 percent of its attention on the problem because 90 percent of its attention is consumed by things like how to change magazines, which firing positions to select, how to set up the machine gun and how to talk on the radio.

On the other hand, an elite unit can focus 90 percent of its attention on unexpected problems because performing basic tasks has become second nature and automatic. Through training, an elite unit has eliminated the controllable variables to simplify the overall equation and free maximum bandwidth for the most difficult problems. Thus, the best way to prepare for uncertainty is not to focus on the uncertainty itself but rather to focus on everything else so the equation will be simplified when the big problem shows up.

This concept also applies to the operational and strategic levels of war. For example, the most complex problem facing U.S. forces during the second Iraq war was likely the sectarian divisions within the country. Regardless of whether this problem was solvable, the United States would have had a much better chance at solving it had U.S. forces first eliminated distractions caused by the simpler, more controllable problems such as the unsecure border with Iran.[1] However, military planners largely neglected the border problem initially, making it easy for hostile forces to smuggle weapons, explosives and personnel into Iraq. As a result, America lost an opportunity to secure an early win that it was well-equipped to achieve.[2] The U.S. military possessed a myriad of platforms, sensors and mobile forces that may have been able to secure the border effectively.[3]

Regardless of whether the border issue was considered the top priority, in some cases leaders should prioritize the easily controllable problems even when they are not the most important problems. The resulting simplification of the equation will free up more bandwidth to focus on the harder problems. In addition, even small victories in warfare have a positive effect on friendly momentum and a reciprocal negative effect on the enemy. For all of these reasons, focusing on the controllable factors first tends to offer the greatest positive result.

Searching for Dysfunction with the Spot Check Method

Identifying the difference between mistakes and dysfunction and understanding the importance of prioritizing controllable factors indicate what leaders should be looking for when searching for correctable dysfunction within their organizations. What is the best method for actually conducting this search? As stated, many organizations suffer from a form of blindness that prevents them from recognizing their own dysfunction. A common excuse is that it is difficult to measure functionality or readiness across large organizations.[4] This excuse is invalid. Measuring functionality of a large organization is relatively easy using the "spot check" method.

If an infantry platoon leader wants to know if all 40 subordinates in his/her platoon have full canteens, there is no time to physically check every one. Instead, the platoon leader tells the squad leaders to check, who in turn tell their team leaders to check. Once every soldier is checked, team leaders report to the squad leaders, who report to the platoon leader. However, even if the squad leaders report that all canteens are full, a good platoon leader will still conduct a few random spot checks of individual soldiers. If the 3 or 4 soldiers the platoon leader checks all have full canteens, then the platoon leader has verified to the best of his/her ability that all canteens in the platoon are full.

However, the critical point is that if the platoon leader finds a single empty canteen, the response is not only to tell that one soldier to fill the canteen and assume the rest are full. The logic behind the spot check is that one deficiency suggests the possibility of other deficiencies. Therefore, if the platoon leader finds one canteen empty, he/she must take serious remedial action to address a possible systemic breakdown in discipline. The spot check has identified a possible dysfunction.

The spot check method applies to all levels of warfare, not only to platoon leaders checking for empty canteens. Good leaders are less likely to be blind to their own dysfunction because they are constantly looking for it, spot-checking subordinates on a regular basis. A leader should not remain isolated within the higher levels of command, but must regularly "troop the line," engaging with subordinates at all levels to gain the most comprehensive understanding of the force's strengths and weaknesses. Brigade commanders can spot-check subordinate battalions by preparing surprise tests and exercises for company commanders. Political-level leadership can spot-check strategic planners by asking to see strategic plans and organizing realistic wargames and simulations. The critical point when conducting spot checks is to remember that one deficiency suggests the possibility of other deficiencies.

The Error of Viewing Dysfunction as Empirical Law

Another likely reason many leaders are blind to dysfunction is that misinterpretations of military wisdom have inadvertently assigned dysfunction the status of an empirical law. This causes leaders to view dysfunction as an inevitable, unavoidable reality that is built in to the very nature of warfare. This phenomenon is possibly best encapsulated by the overused and tragically misunderstood paraphrase of Helmuth von Moltke the Elder, chief of the Prusso-German General Staff from 1857 to 1887.[5] Moltke is often misquoted as saying, "no plan survives first contact with the enemy." This quote has been uttered by countless soldiers from general to private as an excuse for dysfunction and incompetence.

Moltke's actual quote is more nuanced. In his work On Strategy of 1791, he says, "No plan of operations extends with any certainty beyond the first contact with the main hostile force."[6] Obviously, this quote is designed as a caution against overly rigid planning, not a suggestion that planning is useless or impossible. Also, the quote does not deny that planning is critical during all of the essential phases of preparation and deployment leading up to contact with the enemy. Most military professionals will agree that the preliminary moves that set the conditions for battle are often the most critical.

Thus, this tragic misinterpretation of Moltke's wisdom has given countless leaders an excuse for why their nonexistent or sloppy plans inevitably failed. Preeminent military theorist Carl von Clausewitz's concepts of "friction" and the "fog of war" are often equally misinterpreted.[7] There is a sense that bungling and stupidity are unavoidable and it is impossible to execute a seamless operation that runs according to plan. Studying history, there were many well planned, well executed operations in which "hell" did not break loose. For example, the meticulously planned 1940 German Airborne assault on Fort Eben-Emal in Belgium achieved almost flawless results with very few complications.[8]

While flawless execution is certainly rare and the exception to the rule, it is by no means unattainable and is still a realistic goal to strive for. Even the best plan can go awry. Indeed, preparation for the unexpected deserves the status of an empirical law of warfare. The error lies rather in the assumption that the effects of uncertainty and friction cannot be mitigated or managed. If an unexpected storm causes an airborne operation to unravel, that is truly an example of uncertainty or friction. However, when a squad leader fails to conduct pre-combat inspections and half of the squad goes into battle with no ammunition, or when a strategic planner fails to develop contingency plans, that is not friction; that is dysfunction.

Furthermore, even in the truly unavoidable cases like the unexpected storm, there is much planning and preparation a leader can to do mitigate the effects of such surprises. As noted earlier, a defining feature of an elite unit is that it controls the controllables so that when friction strikes, maximum bandwidth remains free to focus on the unexpected; all the other variables are taken care of. Dysfunction is not inevitable and not an empirical law, but rather an inexcusable and curable malady. Once dysfunction is recognized and identified, the next step for curing dysfunction is to diagnose the dysfunction.

STEP 2: DIAGNOSE THE DYSFUNCTION

Recognizing the presence of dysfunction using the spot check method is only the first step. If spot checks identify a dysfunction, the next step is to determine the scope and possible source of the dysfunction. To understand why this is important, an analogy may be useful. If archeologists are trying to excavate a large, oddly shaped object, it will be difficult to pull it from the ground without digging out the entire thing. Without seeing the entire object, it is impossible to identify the appropriate "lift point" or "leverage point" upon which to apply effort.

To make the task of excavation easier, the first step is to dig out the entire object to fully appreciate its size and shape, and then decide where to grasp it. Metaphorically speaking, this is the purpose of the diagnostic step. The process of diagnosis reveals the complete scope, potential source and nature of the problem and therefore helps illuminate the leverage points where applied effort leads to the greatest degree of positive change.

Returning to the empty canteen example, the proximate cause of an empty canteen is most likely that leaders did not conduct proper pre-combat checks. However, how deep does the dysfunction go, and what is its true nature? Is the problem that there are no standard procedures for conducting pre-combat checks within the company?

Or is the deeper problem that the value of checks and inspections is not emphasized in training schools? On an even deeper level, is the established doctrine for conducting pre-combat checks flawed across the entire force?

Examining this canteen example makes it clear that dysfunction can relate to numerous factors, including unit-level procedures, training, doctrine, recruitment, strategy, or choices regarding equipment and technology. Dysfunction is essentially an infection that can spread to multiple components of the military system or machine. Therefore, to accurately diagnose dysfunction, it is useful to have a functional model for how the military system works as a whole. Such a model is provided by the diagram on the opposite page and is repeated on each of the following page spreads so the reader need not flip back and forth to reference the diagram while reading through the section. The text has also been rotated 90-degrees to make it easier to reference the diagram while reading.

A Framework for Combat Performance Enhancement

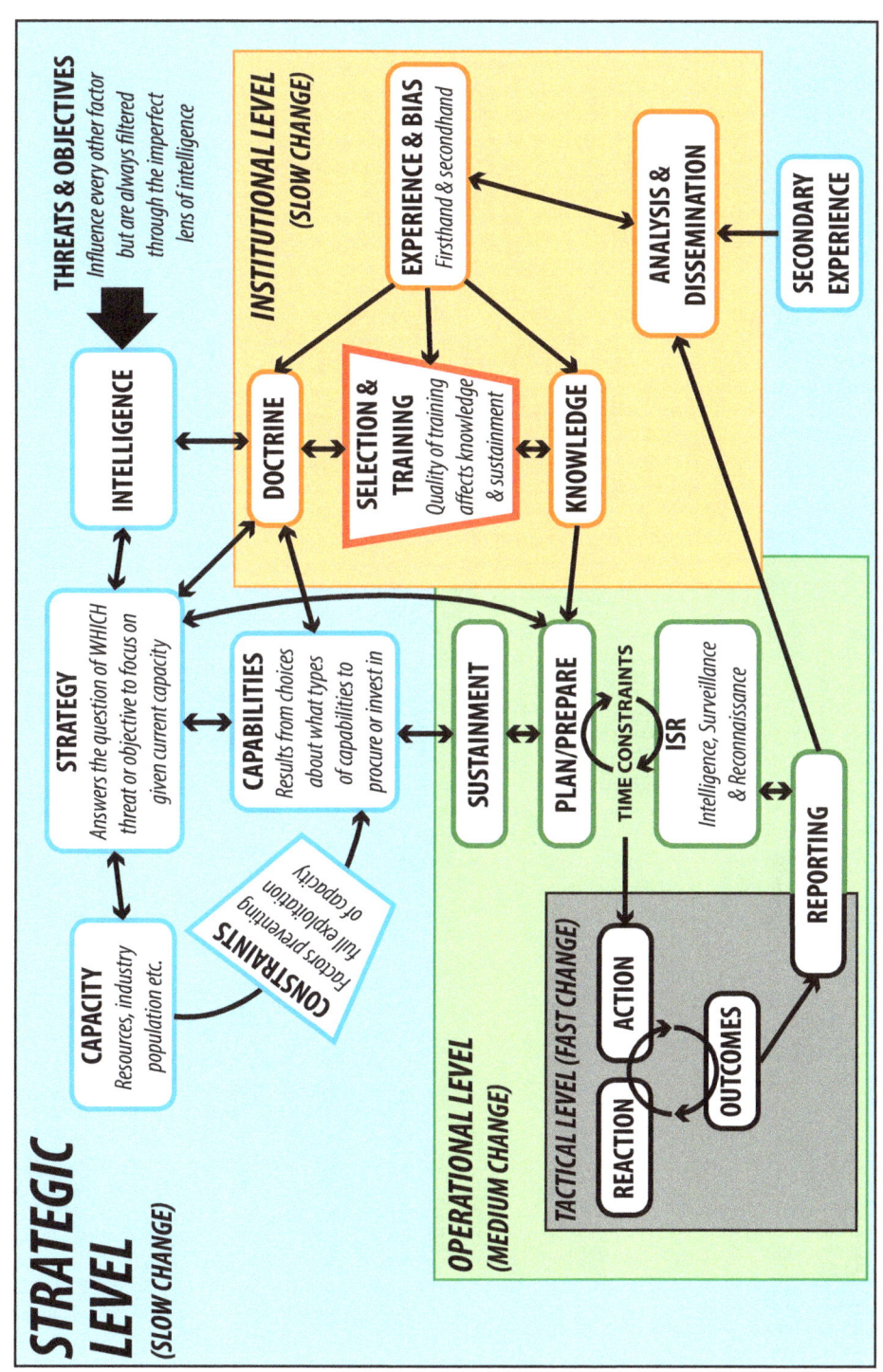

16   *Winning the Fight*

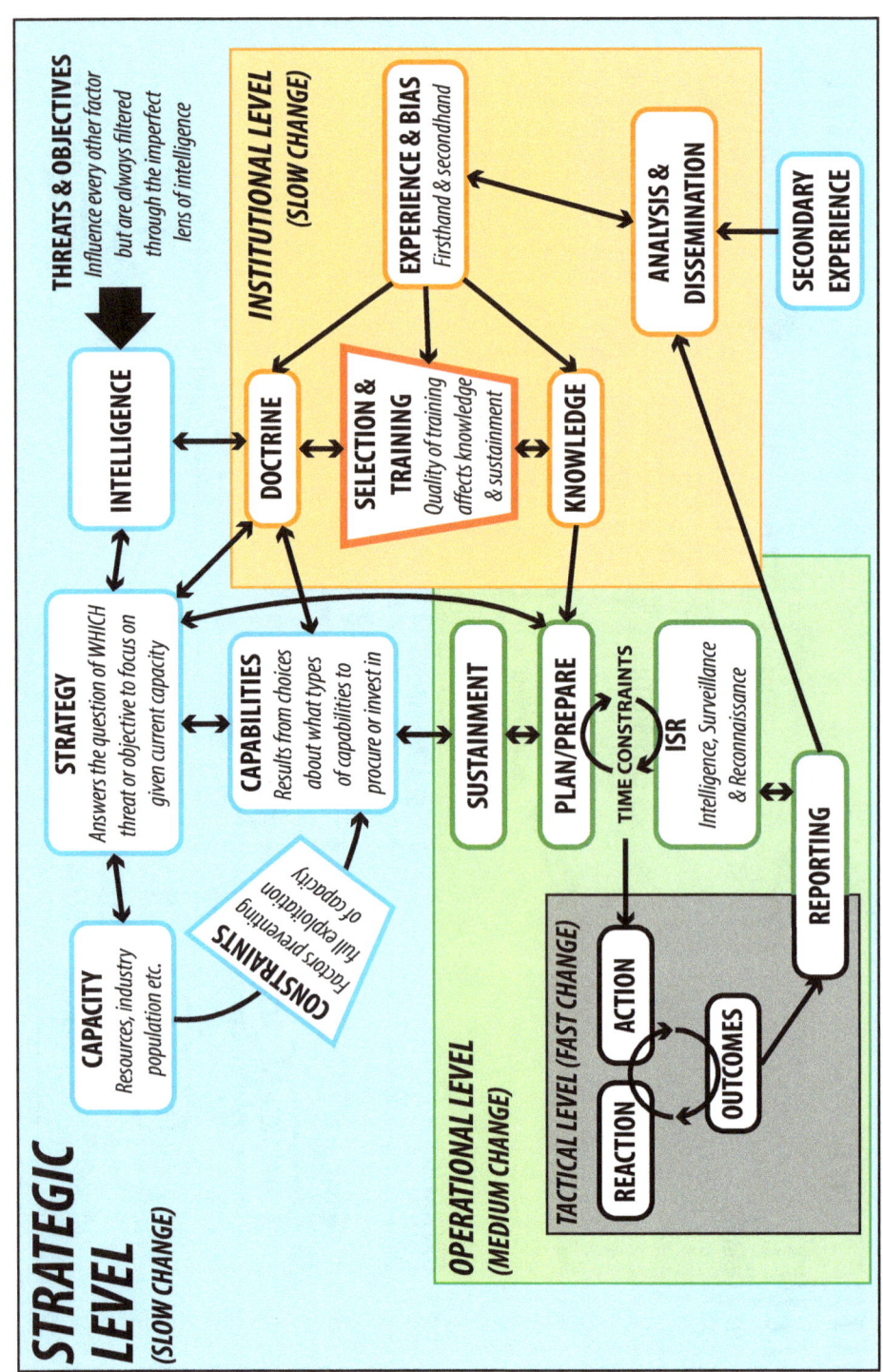

A Framework for Combat Performance Enhancement

Functional Model for the Military Machine

What this book refers to as the "functional model" for the military machine provides a simplified but complete depiction of all aspects of warfare. While the model might appear confusing or intimidating at first glance, it is surprisingly simple and intuitive when viewed in the context of the logical flow of military operations. The functional model is useful because it is very generalized, allowing it to serve as a simplified framework for thinking about warfare more deeply. Most importantly, it provides a context for diagnosing the nature and scope of dysfunction. Just as a map of the organs and systems of the human body can help a doctor understand the source and spread of a disease or infection, the functional model can help military professionals identify the source and spread of dysfunction

In the functional model, the three levels of war (strategic, operational and tactical) are depicted, along with an additional "institutional" level. While the institutional or organizational level of war is discussed by many scholars, it has yet to be incorporated with the other three commonly referenced levels of warfare. For this model, there are four levels of warfare: strategic, institutional, operational and tactical.

Rather than being stacked in a hierarchical configuration, the levels are arranged within one another. This is a more useful and realistic way to depict the true nature of the levels of war. In truth, there is no separation between the strategic, operational and tactical levels of war, and one level is not "above" another. Rather, everything in the tactical level is also relevant to operational art and strategy. Everything in the operational level is also relevant to strategy.

The same does not apply in the opposite direction. While everything tactical is also strategic, there are elements of the strategic level that are purely strategic and do not overlap with tactics. However, as the functional model displays, even elements that do not overlap are ultimately

18 *Winning the Fight*

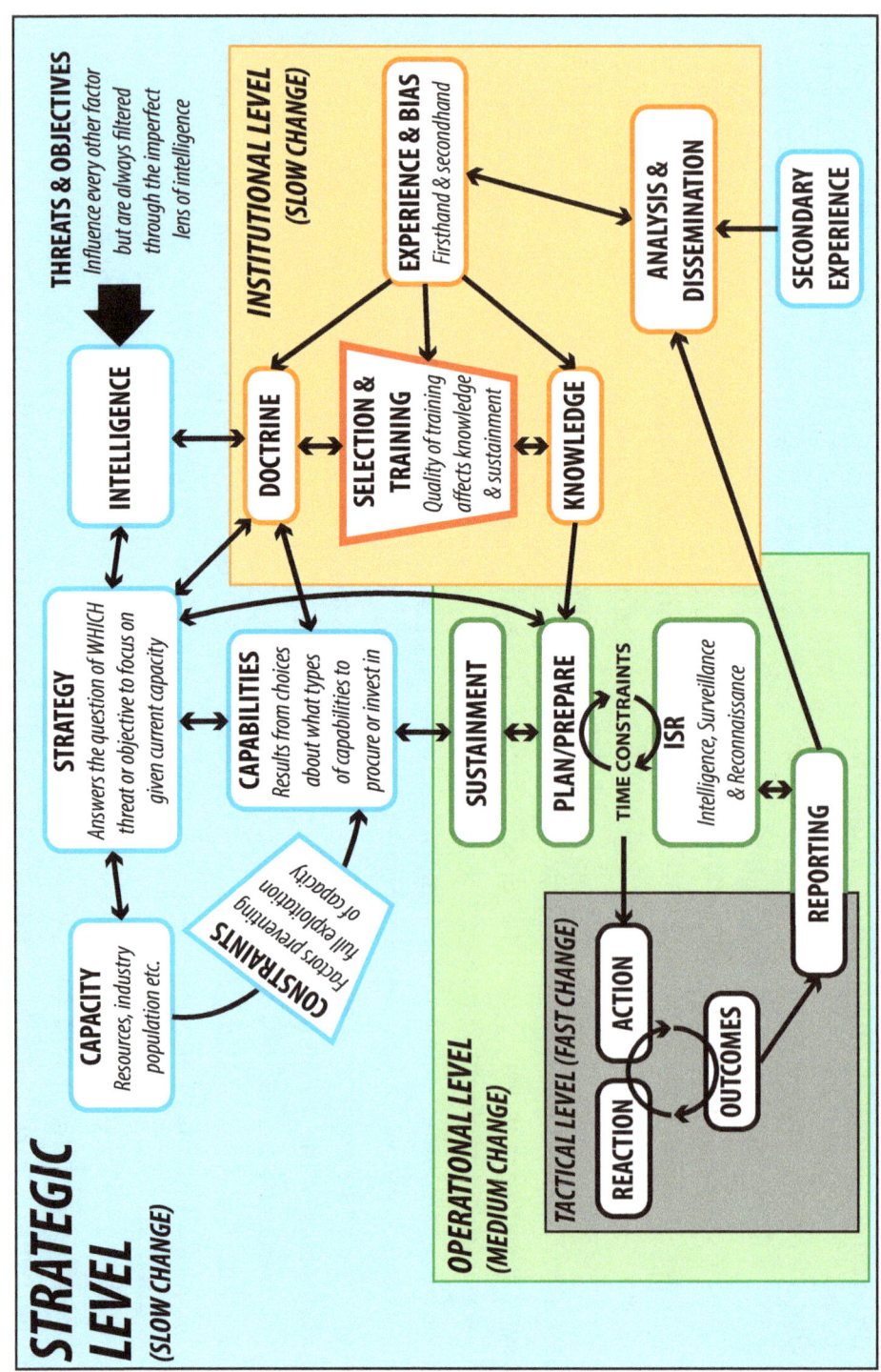

connected, as demonstrated by the arrowed lines. The arrows on the lines are also significant. An arrow from A to B means "A influences B" while a two-sided arrow between A and B means "A and B influence each other."

Looking at the levels of war in this way helps avoid the problem of narrowly labeling an event or problem as "tactical" or "strategic" and overlooking the overlapping and interconnected nature of all levels of war. Each level is also assigned a rate of change. This reflects how long it takes to institute change or foster adaptation at each level. Obviously, implementing change and adaptation at the tactical level is the quickest. Thus, in attempting to affect change by applying effort to the leverage points described earlier, effort applied at the tactical level often yields the quickest results.

However, change at the tactical level often provides the most superficial and shortest-lived cure. In some cases, applying a tactical "band-aid" will not be sufficient and the problem must be addressed further back along the causal chain through implementing changes to operational plans, training, doctrine or strategy. It is also useful to consider change and adaptation in this way because in some cases, there will not be enough time to apply the ideal cure at the appropriate level. Knowing how long various cures will take to implement is extremely useful in many situations.

The actual logical flow of the functional model is fairly intuitive. Words in **bold** relate to the various blocks on the diagram. The first objective is to develop a **strategy** that answers the question of which threat or priority to focus on, given current **capacity** of national resources. Before capacity can be applied on the battlefield, it must first funnel through the **constraints** imposed by factors such as politics, society and the specific situation. The resulting **capability** includes everything from the size of the force to the type of its weapons.

It is also important to remember that every element in the functional model is changeable and every element affects the others around it. For example, Japanese strategic planners prior

Winning the Fight

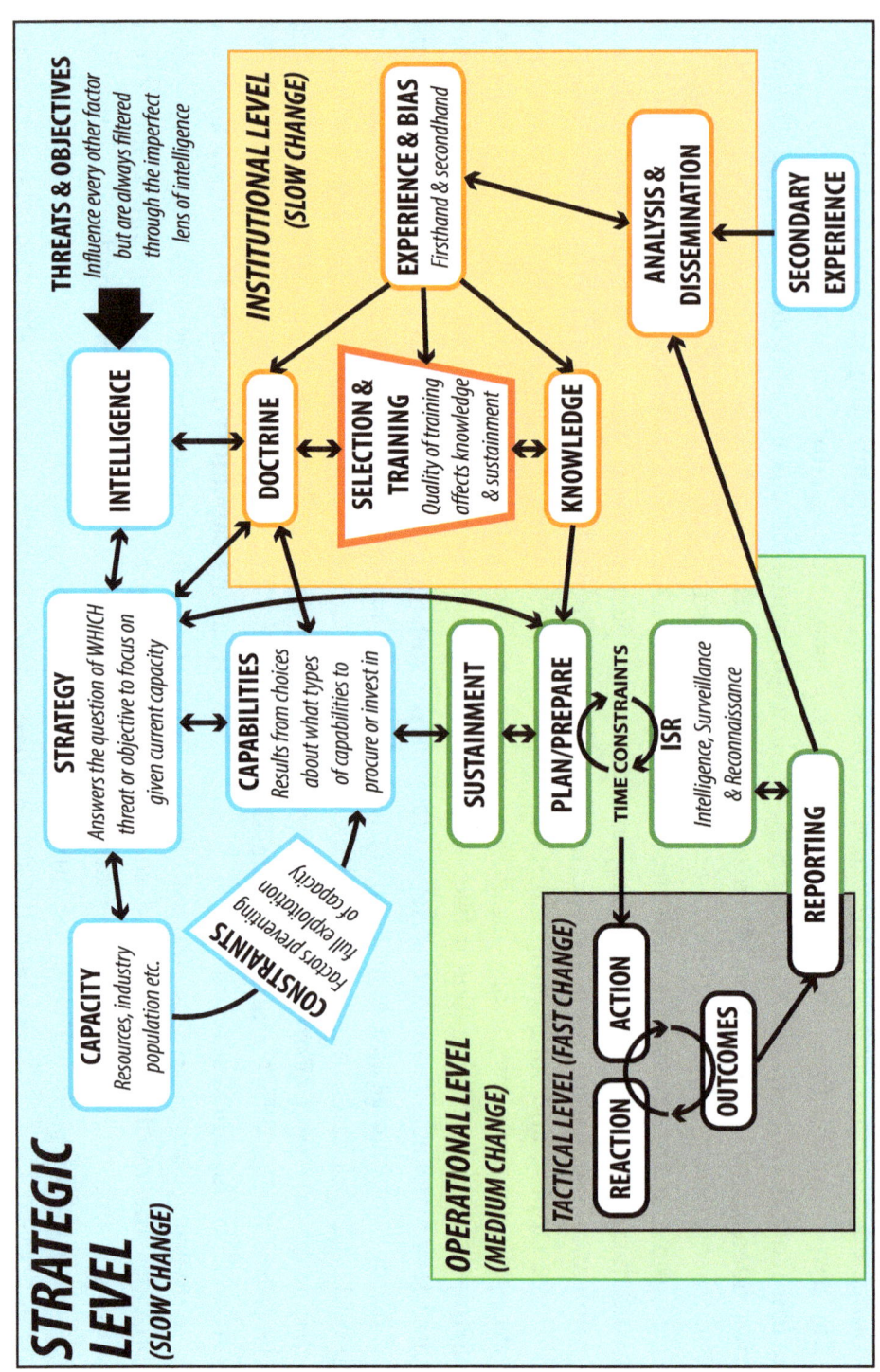

to the Second World War recognized Japan's lack of **capacity** in terms of material resources. However, they realized that this capacity was not unchangeable and went on to develop a **strategy** to conquer territory in order to expand their national **capacity**.[9]

Many factors including **strategy, intelligence** and organizational culture drive the development of **doctrine**.[10] However, since the arrows go both ways, existing **doctrine** also influences how military personnel approach **strategy, intelligence** and the development of new **capability**. Doctrine, however, is meaningless without dissemination and **training**.[11] The quality of training determines the resulting **knowledge** absorbed and retained by the force. Sound doctrine but poor training can have only limited positive effects.

Selection and training are inextricably linked. First, training is not limited to field exercises but rather includes everything a military professional does over the course of his/her career. Training by nature is oriented toward learning and performance evaluation. Thus, the result of any training activity, either formal or informal, is also a selection process, formally or informally. Selection is not solely about choosing the best candidates for elite units, but also includes selecting personnel for promotion or selecting units to serve as the main effort of an operation.

The **selection and training** block by necessity also includes evaluation and sustainment efforts. All of these elements are essential to building a high level of professional **knowledge** within the force. Even when doctrine is sound and training is effective, knowledge will soon atrophy if it is not systematically evaluated and sustained.[12]

Selection and training is outlined in red because it is the most critical part of the machine. No one is born knowing how to do something. Every action taken within a military force had to be trained or learned at some point. Soldiers must be trained to do everything from gathering and analyzing intelligence to providing sustainment services. Trainers must even be trained how to

22 *Winning the Fight*

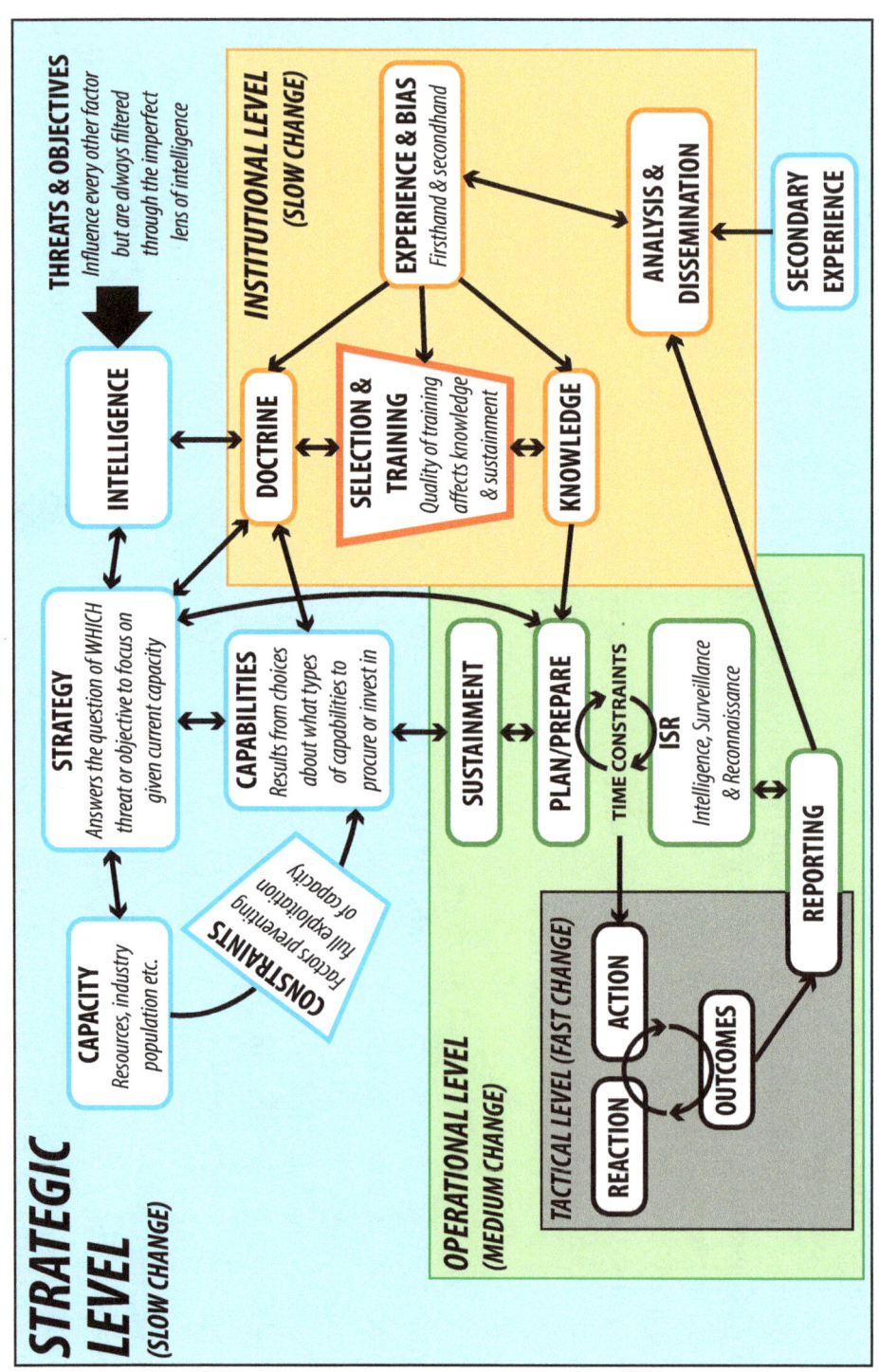

A Framework for Combat Performance Enhancement

train others, and doctrine writers must be trained to write doctrine.[13] Those soldiers also must be selected to fill their given jobs and evaluated on their performance. Thus, selection and training, more than any other factor in the functional model, permeates every aspect of the military machine.

The **knowledge** output from **doctrine** and **training**, good or bad, is what the force takes with it to the battlefield. This knowledge drives operational **planning and preparations**, which are nested in the current strategy. **Planning and ISR** (intelligence, surveillance and reconnaissance) form a never-ending cycle. Initial reconnaissance provides the basis for tentative plans. However, once the planning process begins, it will identify intelligence gaps that become intelligence requirements and drive further reconnaissance planning. The results of reconnaissance lead to changes in the plan that in turn produce even more intelligence requirements, which call for additional reconnaissance and surveillance.

This cycle would go on forever if not for **time constraints**. The intelligence picture is never perfect and at some point, leaders must execute the plan. Planning is also influenced and constrained by ongoing **sustainment** efforts (primarily logistics), which are a function of the force's overall **capabilities** and in turn derive from national **capacity**. Plans are also influenced by **reporting** from ongoing operations.

Finally, the **plan** is implemented through **action** that invariably provokes an enemy **reaction** and leads to an **outcome**. This outcome must be accurately observed and accurately **reported** back to leaders in a timely fashion, then filtered through the existing **ISR** picture to drive new decisions and modifications to **plans**.[14] At the institutional level, these reports also must be passed backwards for **analysis and dissemination** to the rest of the force. This is how battlefield learning should take place.[15]

It is important to realize that lessons learned can also come from **secondary experience**. A professional force will not only learn from its

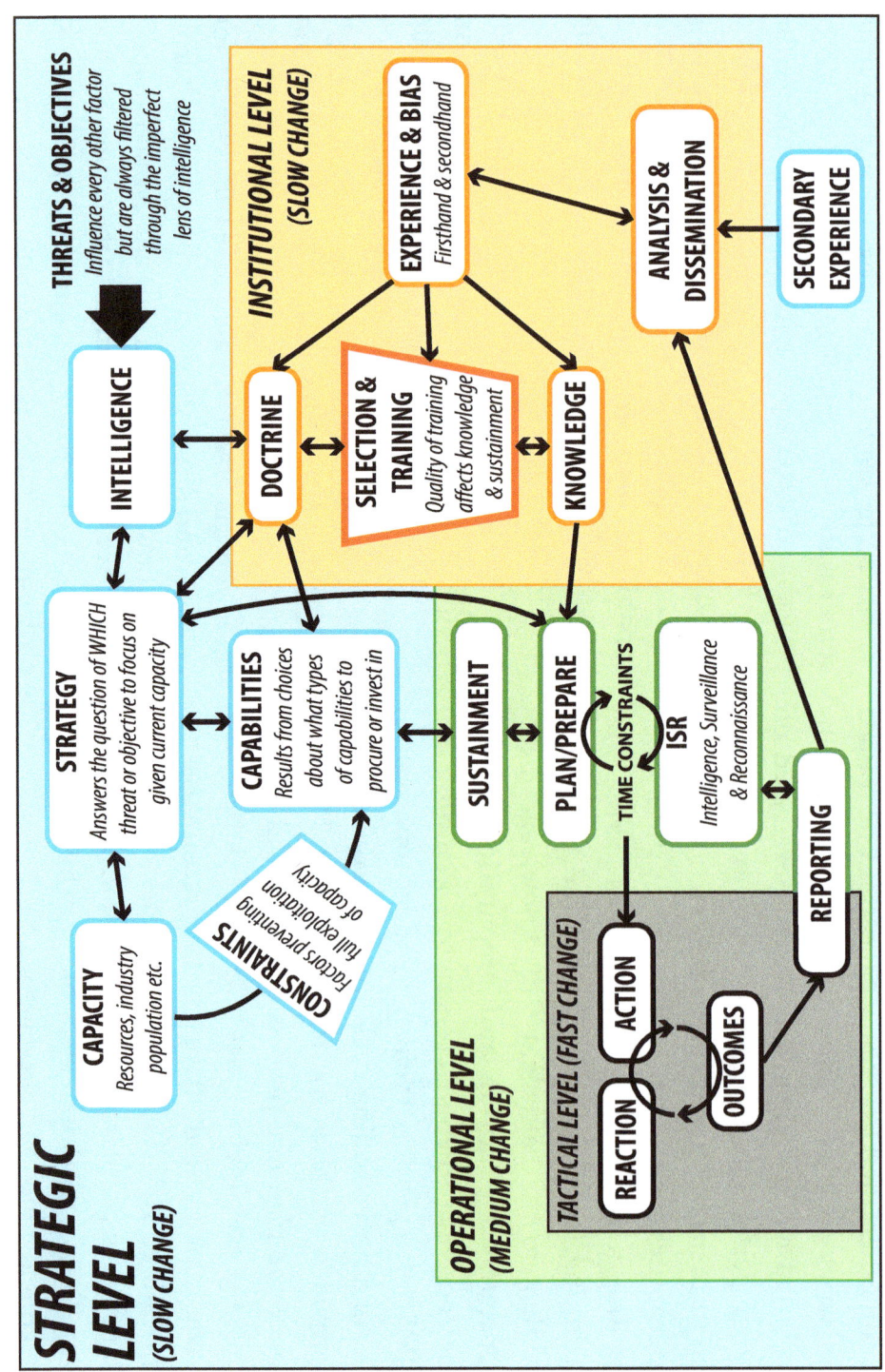

A Framework for Combat Performance Enhancement

training and **knowledge**.[16] Critical flaws relating to experience and bias, such as overconfidence, narrow-mindedness and institutional inertia, can prove to be some of the most insidious problems for a military force.

own experience, but also will try to learn from the experience of other forces in other sectors, theaters or wars. Any analyzed and disseminated lessons must pass through the filter of **experience and bias** before they convert into **doctrine**,

26 *Winning the Fight*

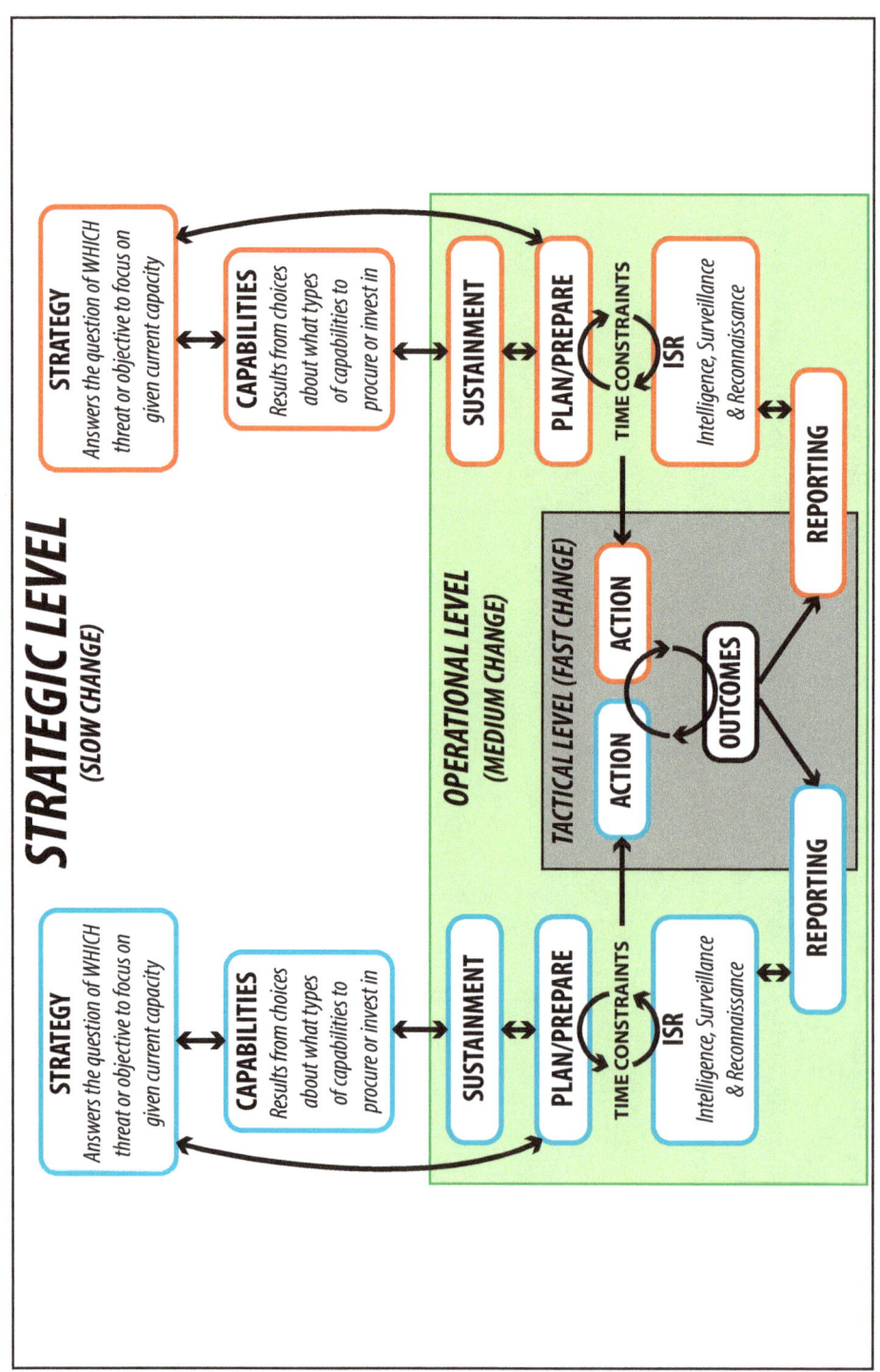

A Framework for Combat Performance Enhancement

The first illustration of the functional model is only one side of a two-sided diagram. This second, two-sided illustration more accurately depicts the way the model works in reality. Note that some blocks have been removed to simplify the diagram. Ultimately, war is a competitive activity. Everything that one side has to do, the other side also has to do. The functional model is general enough so that the military systems of most nations roughly conform to it, though the specific nature of strategy, capacity, constraints, capability, doctrine and training can vary widely.

It is also critical to realize that the two adversarial systems interact only at the tactical level. Any operational or strategic action must ultimately manifest itself at the tactical level to become relevant. This places an increased importance on the tactical level of war, which is often considered less important than the strategic and operational levels.

The reason for this bias within the United States military likely derives from the simplified historical narrative that the Western Allies won the Second World War by applying a superior strategy against a strategically inept but tactically superior Germany. The moral of the story, which everyone has heard, was that you could win the battle but lose the war. This lesson was again reinforced by the experience of Vietnam, where the claim of tactical effectiveness plagued by strategic indecision served to assuage the shame of American failure.[17]

In reality, neither of these historical simplifications is particularly accurate or useful. In fact, they have led to a dangerous de-emphasis of the tactical level of warfare that can only be detrimental in the long run. The tactical level of war is critically important because it is the only level where actual change in the friendly/enemy competitive equation can take place.[18]

Tactics are where the "rubber meets the road." All that is required to render the fastest, most powerful car completely useless is to rub off the tire treads and place it on a sheet of ice. The most powerful engine or machine in the world cannot generate any actual results in terms of speed or performance if there is no contact or traction between the wheels and the surface of the earth. This is not to say that other factors such as the power of the engine are unimportant; rather, the power of the engine must pass through the capacity of the tires to produce traction. Likewise, tactics act as the final filter and chokepoint for the entire military machine depicted in the functional model.

Another critical question regarding the functional model relates to the notable absence of two absolutely critical elements in warfare: leadership and wargames/exercises. These two critical elements are actually not absent, but rather infuse the entire functional model. If the model represents the configuration and design of the military machine, leadership is the actual material or fiber the machine is made of. Essentially, the machine is made of people, and the quality of the people and leaders making up the machine is ultimately the single most decisive factor leading to success or failure.

Another way to think about leadership's relation to the functional model is that key leaders inject themselves at certain blocks or arrows within the diagram to cause either positive or negative effect. For example, British General Bernard Law Montgomery would chiefly insert himself into the planning, training and sustainment blocks as a booster or accelerant.[19] Adolph Hitler, infamous for his strategic blunders, would blanket the entire strategic level as a blocker or inhibitor. When considering the effect of leaders, it is critical to remember that they all must interact with the system at different points and levels, positively or negatively. It is also important to remember that the same leader may exert positive and negative influence simultaneously at different points in the system.

Where do wargames and exercises fit into the functional model? Wargaming is not part of the model itself but rather involves an actual physical exercise of the machine under artificial circumstances. It is widely accepted by many historians and experts, including the revered Sir Michael Howard, that improving a military force without the audit of battle is extremely difficult.[20] Realistic wargames, at all levels, provide the best possible remedy to this problem. A wargame involves creating a fictional enemy and exercising the military machine against it. Just as in real warfare, the lessons learned and the outputs of wargame results can help influence doctrine, training and knowledge.

Diagnosing Dysfunction Along a Causal Chain

Once a dysfunction is recognized and examined in the context of the functional model, the shape of the dysfunction will generally form a casual chain that runs along one or more lines through the functional model diagram. There will often be a proximate cause, the cause that is closest to the negative outcome itself, and a root cause that lies farthest from the outcome. There may be other causes in between that form the causal chain. Returning to the example of the empty canteens, the proximate cause would be a failure to conduct pre-combat checks; the root cause might go deeper into problems regarding training, doctrine or even military culture.

A good historical example can be found in John Nagl's Learning to Eat Soup with a Knife, which discusses reasons for the failed U.S. counterinsurgency effort in Vietnam and compares the U.S. failure to British success in Malaya. Nagl identifies the proximate cause for the failed U.S. counterinsurgency effort in Vietnam as an overreliance on a conventional, attritional approach to warfare. Having determined this proximate cause, the next question is, "Why did the U.S. take a conventional, attritional approach?" Nagl answers this question as well, explaining that organizational/doctrinal stubbornness rejected new concepts for counterinsurgency warfare.[21]

The next step down the causal chain asks the question, "Why was the organization stubborn?" Nagl answers this question by pointing to U.S. military culture and the experiential bias developed during the Second World War and Korea.[22] Essentially, behind every cause there is often a deeper cause. These causes form a causal chain leading from the proximate cause back to the root cause.

Causal chains are particularly important because the outcome of a given campaign or battle is actually the product of chains of events stretching back many years. When considering why a general in the Second World War made a specific mistake, the answer relates to a myriad of past events including the general's previous combat experiences, the quality and focus of his training before the war, who his instructors were, and the curriculum when he attended officer school as a young lieutenant. The timing of changes in military doctrine and technology at various points in the general's career is also relevant. The difficulty lies in mapping all of these various inputs in a way that is not overly complicated and provides useful insights for implementing changes in current operations.

The Importance of Considering Multiple Influences

In diagnosing dysfunction along a causal chain, it is critically important to understand that chains are rarely linear, and that there can often be multiple causal chains that lead to a single outcome. For example, one criticism of Learning to Eat Soup with a Knife was Nagl's failure to account for other potential explanations for why the British succeeded in Malaya while the U.S. failed in Vietnam.

For example, Nagl does not focus on the fact that the Malayan insurgency was executed by an ethnic Chinese minority with limited popularity among the general population.[23] He also does not focus on the Malayans' operational and strategic inferiority to the Vietcong or the notable absence of negative media coverage in Malaya as compared with other revolutionary conflicts.[24] Any of these factors, rather than solely U.S. organizational inflexibility, could explain Nagl's observations.

There are nearly always multiple explanations for a single phenomenon; more importantly, all the explanations generally possess some validity. Did the U.S. win the Gulf War because the U.S. Army was good or because the Iraqi Army was bad? The answer is almost certainly a combination of both. This highlights the critical step of determining which causal chains are the most critical or relevant. This prioritization of causes must rest upon sound logic. Nagl's book might have been more convincing had he explained why organizational inflexibility was more critical than local support, guerrilla competence, or media coverage.

Which Cause Is Most Critical? Which Is Most Changeable?

Diagnosing a problem is such a compelling task that it is easy to ignore whether diagnostic efforts are actually useful in any way. For example, if Nagl determined that the U.S. experiential bias from past wars was the root cause for the failure in Vietnam, that would not offer anything very useful to the practitioner seeking to affect change on the ground. After all, it is impossible to travel back in time to change the experience and culture of the U.S. Army, and cultural transformation typically takes many years. So, the revelation that the cause for U.S. failure in Vietnam was the result of decades of cultural programming would have been of little practical use.

When attempting to solve real-world problems or studying historical cases for professional education, what the practitioner is truly looking for is not the causes that were the most critical but rather the causes that were the most changeable. Therefore, from the practitioner's perspective, the most important question about the Vietnam case study is not "Why did the U.S. fail?" but rather "What could the U.S. realistically have changed, without the benefit of hindsight, that might have altered the outcome?" The same principle applies to any historical case study, from the failure to anticipate the Japanese attack on Pearl Harbor to the failure to predict the terrorist attacks on 9/11. The critical question that can help improve performance in the future is "What might we have done differently that could have altered the outcome?" Answering this question provides the basis for the next step in the process: prescribing specific actions to repair the dysfunction.

Step 3: Prescribe Specific Actions to Repair Dysfunction

As noted, the diagnostic process aims to map the nature and scope of the dysfunction along causal chains, using the functional model as a reference. The next step is to identify not which causes are the most critical, but rather which are the most changeable. Identifying the most changeable causes or factors provides the "leverage point" against which applied efforts have the greatest positive impact. If leaders devote effort, resources or funding to repairing a dysfunction or solving a problem without first identifying this leverage point, the results may be disappointing and prove wasteful.

Many military leaders fail to identify the correct leverage point to affect positive change and thus unintentionally focus efforts in an ineffective direction. In other cases, they may choose an action or remedy that does not actually do anything or have any real effect on the level of dysfunction either way. When leaders choose to apply effort in the wrong direction, the mistake usually takes one of three forms. First, leaders prescribe solutions that are too general, making them difficult to enforce, measure and translate into positive results. Second, leaders prescribe solutions that are too narrow or specific. Such solutions cannot effectively adapt to multiple contingencies and are easily overcome by enemy adaptation. Third, leaders unknowingly continue to apply ineffective solutions because of faulty or limited metrics of success.

The first error, applying a solution that is too general, occurs with tragic frequency in modern military organizations. Simply holding a conference on a subject, creating new departments or new working groups, adding additional layers of bureaucracy, or publishing new studies that few people read likely will not have much impact in terms of reducing dysfunction or improving performance. More importantly, organizations rarely develop or implement effective means of measuring the efficacy of such solutions. When organizations frequently turn to these superficial solutions, it is a sign that leaders are more concerned with "appearing" to do something than they are with actually solving problems or eliminating the dysfunction.

In contrast, Egyptian General Isma'il Ali's reforms prior to the 1973 October War serve as an example of a solution that was too specific. Ali's plan for the October War was so intensely choreographed and scripted that it served to solve only one problem. The plan worked brilliantly for the first several days, allowing the Egyptians to overcome Israel's fixed defenses in a rapid, synchronized advance. However, once the Egyptians ran out of script, they found themselves completely unable to adapt their training and skills to new, unexpected situations. They had solved only one problem-- how to breach the Israeli defenses. Their solution was too narrow to adapt to the uncertain and fluid environment of mobile warfare.[25] Technological solutions to problems frequently fit into this same category, since the new technologies take time to produce, are often easy to counter, and can have limited adaptability in their application to other problems.

An example of a misguided solution based on faulty metrics of success goes back to the U.S. experience in Vietnam. Because the United States military measured success in terms of body counts, it falsely assumed it was making progress when in fact it was not. Thus, the U. S. continued to apply effort and achieve "success" in a direction that was unproductive and often counterproductive.[26]

There are countless examples of ineffective actions taken to counter dysfunction that ultimately have little or no positive effect. Military organizations frequently blame lack of funds, lack of resources or lack of time for their inability to solve problems. In reality, they are often applying their effort in an ineffective direction. If such efforts fail because they are either too broad or too specific, there is logically a leverage point somewhere in the middle where applied effort will have the greatest possible effect.

Identifying Leverage Points in the Context of Time Constraints

The reason leverage points are important in eliminating dysfunction is due to time constraints. As discussed, dysfunction does not usually occur at a single point but is rather the product of several factors laid out in time along one or more causal chains. Thus, a single dysfunction can result from a diverse combination of factors including execution, planning, intelligence, training, doctrine and strategy. When attempting to unravel the chain of dysfunction, if there are no time constraints, there is no reason to be overly concerned with which factor to focus on first. After all, if the dysfunction is the product of many factors, it makes sense to address all of them to achieve the most comprehensive result.

In warfare, time constraints are always present. Even if there appear to be no time constraints, the uncertainty of war makes it impossible to know for sure. Military forces and units do not know when they will next need to put their training and systems to the test. Therefore, there is a sense of urgency when it comes to eliminating dysfunction and improving performance. This sense of urgency makes it very important to apply effort at the leverage point where the effort/outcome ratio is the most favorable, given the time available.

A historical case study that illustrates this point well is the Battle of France in 1940 at the outbreak of the Second World War. Many historians agree that the most decisive causes for the French defeat and German victory stemmed from critical flaws in the rigid and inflexible French military doctrine. If this is the case, for the French to improve their performance in the battle, it would have been logical for them to focus their attention on reforming their doctrine.

However, even if dysfunctions in doctrine were the most critical factor, focusing on doctrine may not have been the best option available to the French military leadership, given the time constraints inherent to warfare. If the French knew they had ten years to prepare

A Framework for Combat Performance Enhancement 35

for the German invasion, focusing on doctrinal reform might have been the best option. However, if the French only had a few months or even a few days to prepare, the most effective leverage point for applied effort might well have changed. After all, it is not realistic to conduct a comprehensive doctrinal overhaul in a short time and in such cases, remedies with more immediate positive outcomes might prove more appropriate.

As we have seen, each block and area within the functional model is associated with a different rate of change. Tactical change is the fastest and easiest. Strategic and institutional change is the hardest and slowest. A more immediate cause for the French defeat, which could have been corrected in a few months or even weeks, was a dysfunction in French planning. The French had no contingency plan for dealing with alternate German courses of action.

The French placed all their eggs in one basket, banking on the certainty of a German attack in the north, through Belgium. The French had ample justification to expect the Germans to attack in the north; that was an honest mistake. However, their failure to at

The German Invasion for France 1940

least consider the alternatives and to develop contingency plans accordingly qualifies as dysfunction. When the German attack came in the south through the Ardennes Forest, the French found themselves completely unprepared, and the lack of a contingency plan made it impossible for them to adapt to the situation. This lack of contingency planning was an obvious oversight that might have been easily fixed had the French identified it.

Therefore, if the French had only a few months or weeks to eliminate dysfunction within their force and the causal chain of dysfunction ran from planning to doctrine, it would have made more sense to focus on addressing the dysfunctions in planning rather than doctrine, because the positive results would have come faster. This is not to say that repairing the dysfunction with planning would have prevented a French defeat, as deeper doctrinal dysfunctions still would have been present. However, given a short time window, focusing on planning could have offered more leverage for efforts that would have had the greatest impact on outcome.

The German Invasion of France 1940

Because it is impossible to know the actual time constraints, it usually wise to apply effort at the leverage point. With only 24 hours in each day, it makes sense for military forces or units to apply effort at the point where they will get the most "bang for their buck," regardless of whether that point addresses the most critical problem or not. It is always possible to go on and address deeper causes later, once the easy fixes are complete. This is similar to how medics treat casualties in the field. The priority is to "stop the bleeding" and address other time-sensitive problems as quickly as possible. Once the casualty is stabilized to some degree, more complex medical procedures can take place later at a hospital. Therefore, even if the best option for the French was to attempt doctrinal reform, it may have made sense for them to fix their dysfunctional plan first, before tackling the more critical doctrinal dysfunction.

It is also relevant to remember that time constraints are not the only reason it makes sense to apply effort at the leverage point, where affecting positive change is the easiest. As noted in an earlier discussion of controllable vs. uncontrollable factors, going for the quicker fixes first also is beneficial because it simplifies the overall equation and frees up bandwidth to focus on more complex problems. This is not to say that leaders should always tackle the easier problems first. There are no fixed rules in warfare. There may be cases when the best option is focusing immediately on the most complex and difficult problem. For example, French leaders in 1940 might have decided to focus on doctrinal reform first if they decided that their doctrinal dysfunction was so critical that it rendered efforts to improve their defensive plan irrelevant. Ultimately, the leader must decide how to allocate time and resources in the most productive way.

Developing Pattern Recognition through Training and Wargaming

When attempting to identify and prescribe specific actions to repair dysfunction, it is generally best to focus on leverage points that will offer the quickest results and the largest "bang for the buck" in terms of effort/outcome ratio. However, there is no foolproof or scientific way to know where these leverage points actually are. Despite the number of mathematical tools and formulas available to analysts, in the end all decisions are made by human beings using logic, creativity and intuition. This is not to say that quantitative analysis cannot be helpful, only that it should be used to inform rather than drive the decision-making process.

How can leaders identify leverage points and choose the best focus of effort if there are no formulas for doing so? The answer lies in the leader's logical and intuitive thinking skills. It is impossible to know to what degree thinking ability is innate and to what degree it can be learned or trained. However, it is clearly possible to improve thinking ability over time through education and training. The cornerstone of this training is developing a capacity for pattern recognition.

There are many detailed, scientific studies that compare intuitive and analytical decision making, examine the nature of expertise, or study the mental components of performance. These studies can provide useful insights. For the practitioner, there is a more streamlined and simplified way to understand the most relevant theme running through these studies. When someone plays a sport he/she has never played before, poor performance is almost inevitable. Conversely, when observing a true master of any sport, someone who makes the most challenging feat appear effortless, that master is almost invariably someone who is intimately familiar with the sport and fluent in the various movements and competencies associated with it.

An individual's familiarity and fluency in a given discipline determines their capacity for pattern recognition. This is not to say that experience is the most important factor, particularly when measured in years. There are combat soldiers with many years of experience who have only conducted a live-fire building clear, combat river crossing, or combined-arms breach a handful of times during their careers. To make matters worse, training exercises are often scripted and unrealistic, meaning that the patterns trainees are recording look nothing like what they will encounter in real combat against a thinking opponent.

Veterans of the Second World War who conducted hundreds building clears, combat river crossings and breaching operations developed a greater capacity for pattern recognition in a few months or years than peacetime military professionals might develop over a lifetime. The relevant factor is not simply years of experience, but rather the nature of that experience and the number of exposures an individual has to realistic scenarios. Average citizens can develop intuitive driving skills in less than a year if they drive every day under varying conditions.

Therefore, the best way to develop pattern recognition in peacetime is to conduct as many realistic training exercises as possible. It is important that these exercises not be scripted and that they force trainees to think and solve unexpected problems under stressful conditions, just as they would in real combat. Scripted, unrealistic training can actually be detrimental to combat performance as it encourages bad habits, inhibits thinking, and sets false expectations about battle.

After repeated exposure to realistic training scenarios, leaders and units will begin to develop a capacity for pattern recognition, a "game sense" that will allow them to identify leverage points quickly though analytical thinking, logic and intuition. If training exercises are too resource intensive, it is possible to achieve many of the same benefits using wargames. Wargames can take many forms, including computer simulations, board games, map drills and tabletop scenarios. Wargames are also a great training resource, because trainees can typically execute many more repetitions of various professional tasks in a wargame than they can in a complex live exercise with many moving parts.

Developing Pattern Recognition with Historical Case Studies

Historical case studies are probably the easiest and least resource-intensive way to improve pattern recognition. Every time a student "thinks through" a historical case study, the activity in the brain is similar to the activity that would manifest if that student was executing the operation in a live training exercise or wargame. It can also prove useful to introduce aspects of wargaming into the historical studies themselves. For example, what would have happened if the French had developed an effective contingency plan in 1940? What if the United States had used a different system for analyzing and disseminating lessons learned in Vietnam? Once students understand the dynamics of a historical battle, it can be useful to wargame various alternative courses of action against live opponents to see how combat performance might have been improved.

The more historical case studies a military professional conducts, the more the usefulness of those studies grows. By analyzing what has worked and what has not worked over the course of many historical case studies, it is possible to identify a common a set of prescriptions or best practices in the form of maxims, processes and causal patterns, including common mistakes to be avoided. As the pattern of best practices develops, it will begin to take the form depicted in the simple chart below.

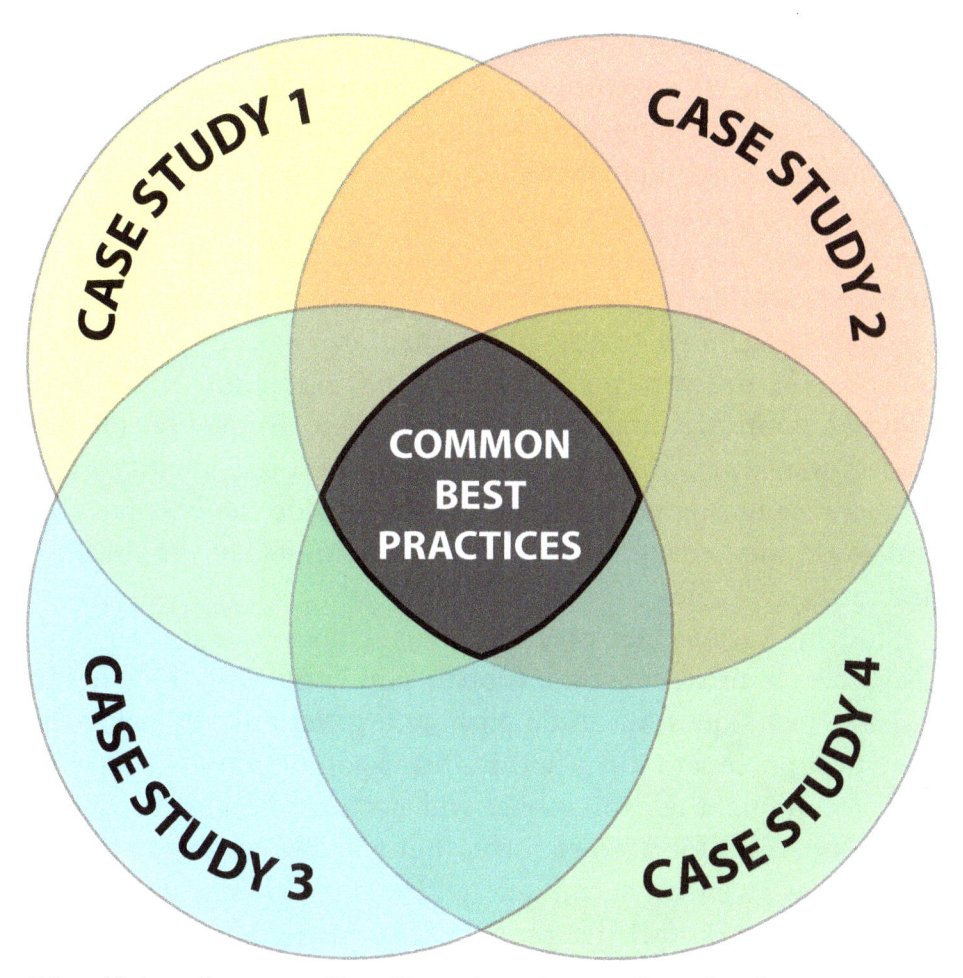

Identifying Common Best Practices Across Case Studies

In the above chart, each colored circle represents the sum of best practices from a case study of a given force in a given campaign. The darkest area in the center represents the best practices or prescriptions common to every case. As the range of data increases, the reliability of these common best practices grows higher and higher.

The areas on the periphery represent practices that worked for the given country in the given campaign but were not present in other examples. These practices must be collected as well, as they may have particular utility in specific situations. Comparing the patterns of the effectiveness or ineffectiveness of specific practices across a range of campaigns will help clarify situations in which such practices might prove useful.

Achieving true mastery in warfare does not only mean knowing the best way to proceed under ideal circumstances, but rather includes knowing the best way to proceed given the limitations of your force and the particulars of the situation. For example, German practices of decentralized planning and execution might have proved less effective in the Soviet Army, where the quality of junior leaders was lower. Thus, a true military expert can identify when a theoretically suboptimal solution will provide the best possible real-world outcome, given the specific constraints of the situation and forces available.

Studying various best practices across countries and campaigns also serves to broaden a professional's familiarity with the range of possible techniques for accomplishing a given task. By using the analytical process to identify the advantages and disadvantages of each technique, the professional will not only be able to choose the best options for his own forces, but will also be able to exploit weaknesses in enemy techniques and forecast enemy actions and reactions. Such knowledge proves useful in combined operations with foreign countries.

Even when opportunities for training and wargaming are limited, rigorous study and contemplation of a wide variety of historical case studies helps develop the capacity for pattern recognition and intuitive decision making, the mark of true professionals.[27] Conversely, if military professionals study only one or two historical scenarios and try to reapply those historical lessons to contemporary conflict, the result can be disastrous. The critique that studying history makes practitioners narrow-minded in their approach to modern problems only applies when the selection and breadth of studies is not sufficiently large or diverse. The best way for a practitioner to study history is not to focus on one or two cases but rather to study as many cases as possible, thinking through each one and identifying their common patterns. Studying numerous examples of what has worked and what has not worked in various situations helps develop an intuitive ability to predict outcomes and choose leverage points.

Measuring Results

The combined wisdom and lessons learned from realistic training, wargaming and historical case studies can help leaders identify the best leverage points to improve performance, repair dysfunction and affect positive change. Once leaders decide how to apply effort and resources, the next critical step is finding the best ways to measure what is working and what is not. As discussed earlier, leaders frequently fail to improve performance or repair dysfunction because they apply an inappropriate solution that simply does not have a positive effect. To make matters worse, leaders often do not even realize that their efforts are ineffective because they have not identified useful metrics for measuring results.

Some modern studies differentiate measures of performance from measures of effectiveness. Essentially, measures of performance determine how well a force is doing something, while a measure of effectiveness measures whether what the force is doing actually has the desired effect. The U.S. might have achieved good performance results in Vietnam in terms of body count, but did that body count prove effective in terms of the desired strategic outcome? The distinction between measures of performance and measures of effectiveness is worth noting; however, getting overly absorbed in the difference between the two can prove confusing and counterproductive.

Trying to develop foolproof, mathematical rules for measuring results is often less effective than simply applying common sense and logical thinking. Measuring results, performance or effectiveness can be very difficult, and it is not always clear which factors to measure. However, the more realistic a unit's wargames, exercises and training scenarios, the easier it is to measure results. Units that win are often doing the right things. Units that lose may be focusing efforts in the wrong area. Once leaders identify a pattern of winning and losing, it is possible to dig deeper and try to find the common practices of the units that are winning and the units that are losing. This can help identify other metrics to predict performance prior to execution.

Metrics that can help measure performance or effectiveness and predict whether a unit will win or lose can take unpredictable forms. Traditional measures such as total training hours, results from predictable or scripted tests, or subjective performance evaluations from superiors are often of limited value. Less traditional metrics can prove more useful and are more likely to identify a correlation between measurable data and favorable results. Below are several nontraditional metrics that are easily measured and have a strong correlation with higher levels of performance and effectiveness.

1. **Are units sharing lessons learned laterally?** The practice of conducting AARs (After Action Reviews) and recording lessons learned from each training exercise or battle is a critical task for any professional military unit. However, just checking whether or not a unit conducts AARs is of limited value, as much of the time AARs are completed hastily and carelessly, and filed away where no one will ever see them again. The most important part of the AAR is actually studying it, reflecting on it and disseminating the lessons learned throughout the force. Therefore, a highly professional unit will ensure subordinate units share AAR results laterally with each other. To test for this, all that is necessary is to ask 2nd Battalion for 1st Battalion's AAR from the most recent training exercise. If 2nd Battalion still has the AAR, knows where to find it and understands its content, that suggests a strong correlation with high performance, effectiveness and success.

2. Do units receive warning before evaluations or exercises? Many military training exercises or performance evaluations are very easy because the participants receive plenty of warning about when the evaluation will take place and what skills will be tested. It is rare to find a unit that uses the pop-quiz model, in which there is no warning of when the evaluation will take place or what will be tested. However, employing the pop quiz has a strong correlation with high performance, effectiveness and success.

3. How much personal time do unit members spend on professional development? It is one thing if unit members spend time on professional development because it is mandatory. When unit members are motivated enough to spend personal time on professional development activities, including professional reading, physical fitness, marksmanship and fighting skills, that is a sign of an outstanding command climate and has a strong correlation with high performance, effectiveness and success. It is also relatively easy to measure how many members of a unit spend a significant amount of personal time on professional development.

4. Are units/leaders able to articulate their own weaknesses? This is very easy to measure and has an overwhelmingly strong correlation with high performance, effectiveness and success. When a leader is simply unable to articulate his/her unit's weaknesses or discuss them in an intelligent way, it is a sign of serious dysfunction, incompetence and lack of self-awareness. Conversely, better units are quite aware of their own weaknesses and can discuss them intelligently from memory, without having to reference any documents.

The metrics above are only a few examples of nontraditional ways to measure performance, effectiveness and chances of success.

Remember that the examples above do not really measure the actual abilities or competencies that lead to success, but rather have a positive correlation with success. In simple terms, units that do "X" tend to win, whereas units that do "Y" tend to lose. Identifying these correlations can be one of the most useful ways to measure results. For example, if new doctrinal or training reforms are causing a noticeable increase in the amount of personal time unit members voluntarily devote to professional development, that is a sign that reforms are having a deep, positive effect on unit performance.

By applying both traditional and nontraditional metrics, it is possible to gain a better understanding of whether applied efforts are having the desired effect. In some cases, leaders might identify a leverage point for repairing dysfunction, but over time, metrics will suggest that a different leverage point will produce more positive results. There is no fixed formula for choosing the best metrics or measurement techniques. Instead, leaders must use logical thinking and common sense.

Step 4: Anticipate Obstacles and Develop Counters

Even after successfully completing steps 1-3, it is still possible to fail. On the battlefield, determining the objective and developing a course of action are easy compared to the difficult task of anticipating the enemy's countermoves. The same applies in any effort to eliminate organizational dysfunction. In some cases recognizing dysfunction, diagnosing dysfunction and identifying the leverage point for repairing dysfunction is relatively simple. However, applying the solution can prove extremely difficult because of unanticipated obstacles and resistance.

Any reform or change will inevitably upset the current balance of organizational power and prove displeasing to certain individuals. Efforts toward positive change may also encounter unanticipated external obstacles or trigger unanticipated conflicts between various competing elements and interests. It is impossible to predict the obstacles to effective change with certainty. However, by using the same type of thinking useful for military planning, it is possible to wargame and anticipate obstacles, and to develop counters to them beforehand.

Summary: From Concept to Application

To summarize the entire process described in the preceding section, the first step calls for recognizing the presence of dysfunction by first differentiating dysfunction from honest mistakes, and understanding that dysfunction is solvable while mistakes are inevitable. This understanding highlights the importance of controlling the easily controllable factors to free up bandwidth to devote to less-controllable factors. The next step is to use the spot check method to identify points of dysfunction within the organizational system, realizing that individual deficiencies can be a sign of larger, systemic dysfunctions.

After recognizing the presence of dysfunction, the next step is to diagnose the scope and causes of the dysfunction using the functional model as a reference. This process generally involves tracing the dysfunction along one or more causal chains running from a proximate cause to a root cause. While it is useful to understand which causes are the most critical, it is generally the causes that are most changeable that provide the best leverage point, the point to which applied effort will offer the greatest positive impact. If leaders fail to identify the leverage point and instead apply a solution that is too broad, too narrow, or ill fitted to the problem, results will likely be unsatisfactory. By instead applying effort at the leverage point, leaders achieve the quickest possible results, which is critical given the inherent unpredictability and time constraints of warfare.

There is no formula for how to identify the best leverage point against which to apply effort. However, by conducting numerous historical and contemporary case studies using the functional model as a reference, it is possible to identify a common set of best practices and causal patterns. Applying the resulting knowledge in realistic training scenarios over time will develop a capacity for pattern recognition that can help leaders identify leverage points to repair dysfunction. Developing effective metrics to measure what is working and what is not can help leaders improve performance even further, and also to identify specific organizational behaviors that have a strong correlation with greater effectiveness.

Finally, while in some cases recognizing dysfunction, diagnosing dysfunction and identifying the leverage point for repairing dysfunction is relatively simple, applying the solution can prove extremely difficult because of unanticipated obstacles and resistance. Any efforts for reform or change will inevitably encounter obstacles, because change upsets the current balance of organizational power and may also trigger unanticipated conflicts between various competing interests. It is impossible to predict these obstacles with certainty, but by using the same type of thinking useful for military planning, it is possible to wargame to anticipate obstacles and develop counters to them beforehand.

The four steps of performance enhancement described above, combined with the functional model for the military machine and the essential practices of wargaming and historical analysis, provide a new way to study any military operation at any level. This approach extracts the information that is most critical for the military practitioner in preparing for future conflicts. While the sequence of logic explained in the preceding section can prove difficult to absorb in a single reading, studying and applying the described practices over time can make the process of performance enhancement more intuitive and easier to grasp.

Providing a complete historical case study to allow readers to walk through each step of the process might seem a useful addition to this book and could better illustrate the concepts and steps described thus far. However, actually applying the four steps of performance analysis is a very involved and detailed process. Conducting a single case study would likely fill a volume twice as long as this book and is therefore beyond its scope. Such "performance focused" historical case studies will be published in future volumes, but to include one in this book would be a departure from the main objective of providing a short, easily digestible guide for practitioners.

Application of the Functional Model

The following section takes the functional model for combat performance enhancement described in the previous section and applies it to various aspects of military operations. Just as the first section attempts to explain how the military machine functions in the most general sense, the following section provides more practical explanations for how to use the machine in different situations.

The order of chapters is relevant and does not necessarily follow the logical order implied by the functional model diagram. While the functional model attempts to show how the machine functions as a whole, the following chapters are organized according to the order that will prove most effective for the practitioner engaged in actual combat. The first chapter is on strategy, providing an overall understanding of how to direct efforts at the highest level in order to offer context for lower-level actions.

The second chapter covers defense. It is logical to start with defense because in any combat situation, at either the tactical or the national level, the first priority must be to secure the force from enemy attack. Even if a force is only half-built and lacking countless other competencies, it cannot hope to rebuild or improve if it is under constant threat of destruction. Thus, the first step is to learn to defend. From this defensive position all other military activities, including offensive planning, can take place.

The third chapter covers intelligence because intelligence drives planning. The fourth chapter discusses planning because planning is necessary for the offensive operations discussed in the fifth chapter. The final chapter is the most important chapter in the book, covering selection and training. Only after understanding how a force is supposed to function and accomplish critical tasks is it possible to develop the best methods for training that force and for selecting the right people to lead it.

It is important to note that several of the following chapters may seem redundant in places. This is intentional for several reasons. First, it is preferable for each chapter to function as a stand-alone reference that practitioners can consult on a case-by-case basis without having to review the entire text. Second, redundancies between chapters highlight the connection points where various parts of the machine overlap or come together, helping the reader achieve better understanding of the big picture. Finally, concepts that surface in multiple chapters are critically important concepts that warrant review and examination in multiple contexts.

It is important to note that the following chapters do not mirror the functional model diagram exactly. One might assume that there would be a subchapter on each individual block of the functional model. However, this would not be very useful, as the critical insights of the functional model stem from examining how the various blocks interact rather than operate in isolation. The reader might also notice that there is no block for "offense" or "defense" on the functional model, but there are chapters on offense and defense. Offense and defense are applications of multiple elements in the functional model, and more useful reference points for a practitioner seeking to develop professional competence. In essence, the goal of the following sections is not to dismantle the machine but rather to understand how the machine works in realistic scenarios.

Finally, much of the discussion in the following chapters will descend to the tactical level and focus on seemingly mundane and trivial details that do not belong in a book that claims to explain warfare as a whole. However, the focus on these details is no accident and is in fact critically important to understanding the reasons why military machines either function or fail to function. Highly respected works on military theory discuss complex concepts such as political/military relations, the nature of war, and the causes of war. While these concepts are certainly important, many more battles and wars were lost because of something as simple as inaccurate reporting. Statistically speaking, a force that knows how to solve the problem of inaccurate reporting through establishment, dissemination and enforcement of standard operating procedures has a better chance of winning than a force that spends too much time contemplating the nature of war.

This book does not seek to drill down to every detail of execution that can lead to success or failure; rather, it seeks to tie higher-level, theoretical or conceptual thinking to the critical aspects and practical truth of war as experienced on the ground, which ultimately has the greatest impact on success or failure. The most competent and prepared force understands the nature of war and also knows how to deliver accurate reports. In reality, the two elements are connected. In order to truly understand the nature of war and the theory of war, it is necessary to understand the details as well as the big picture. The following chapters will not shy away from examining minute operational details in cases when such details can prove useful.

Finally, it is worth noting that there is no chapter covering logistics. While logistics is a critical component of the military machine, it is a very difficult subject to cover in a generalized way. Providing a chapter on logistics that would prove useful to practitioners would require a very long and detailed discussion that is beyond the scope of this book. Future publications will address the nature and problems of logistics in detail.

Strategy

The study and understanding of strategy is plagued by many misconceptions. First, as expressed in the functional model, strategy is not a "level" of war but rather a realm that encompasses all other aspects of war. Strategy is not distinct from tactics and operations. Rather, strategy is the all-inclusive universe that contains operations and tactics. Thus, everything tactical and operational is also strategic. One cannot claim to be a master strategist without also being a master tactician.

A second misconception is that strategists cannot be trained or that teaching strategic thinking is very difficult. In reality, it is the mislabeling of strategy as a distinct and higher realm of thought that contributes to a scarcity of established methods for teaching and practicing strategy. Soldiers at the lowest level need to pass training courses and meet codified standards before leading even a handful of troops on the battlefield. What course or standards assess the strategic competence of the policymakers who make the most critical decisions about our national security?

The same elements of performance enhancement discussed in the first section apply to the strategic realm. It is indeed possible to train strategists. It is possible to measure strategic competence and effectiveness. It is possible to codify certain aspects of the strategic process with the aim of achieving more successful outcomes. These facts become apparent when we examine historical case studies of bad strategy, identify critical elements that were missing, and verify that the inclusion of such elements contributed to success in other cases. This approach produces a clear set of guidelines for increasing the chances of strategic success, while allowing greater bandwidth for creative thinking by controlling the controllables.

The Nine Elements of Strategy

As depicted in the diagram below, any strategy consists of nine elements: four estimates, four calculations and a central theory of victory. The distinction between calculations and estimates is not absolute and intends only, in general terms, to divide the elements that are more quantifiable from those that are less quantifiable. Modern strategic thinking has traditionally focused on the right side of the chart, attempting to use quantitative analysis to drive decisions and predict outcomes. In reality, both sides of the chart are important to developing an effective strategy. As the arrows demonstrate, quantitative analysis must proceed separately but cooperatively with qualitative analysis, and everything must revolve around a single theory of victory.

Theory of Victory

The theory of victory is the most important element in a strategy, and is also the most complex and difficult to define. Generally, the best approach is to begin strategic planning with a tentative theory of victory but to remain prepared to adjust the theory as analysis proceeds on each side of the diagram. Ultimately, for the strategy to be effective, every individual element of the strategy must align with the overall theory of victory.

The theory of victory is a plausible story or narrative of how a conflict will reach a favorable conclusion. There is no specific formula or format for a theory of victory, other than it must

Strategy 57

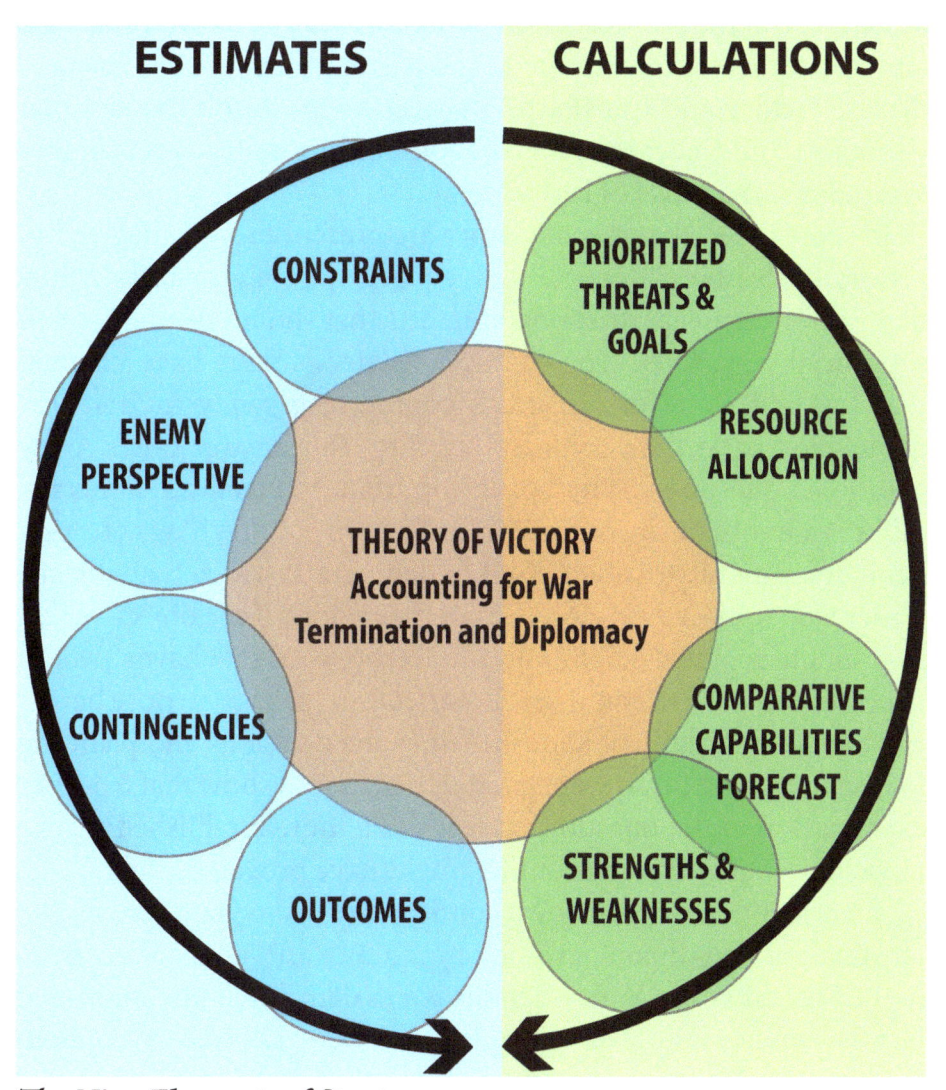

The Nine Elements of Strategy

make logical sense. In many cases, simply asking senior leaders to articulate a theory of victory would have exposed strategic incompetence in past conflicts. For example, Hitler never formally articulated a theory of victory. Exactly what was Hitler trying to accomplish at the political level? What was Hitler's desired end state and how exactly did he hope to get there? When could Germany declare victory and transfer to a peacetime posture? The fact that Germany could never answer these kinds of questions was both a symptom and a cause of bad strategy.

In some cases, theories of victory are present to some degree but prove hopelessly inadequate. Inadequacies usually manifest while digging for the deeper national interests that should lie underneath superficial objectives. For example, leaders might have claimed that the end state for America's counterinsurgency in Iraq was democracy, or at the very least, stability. This answer raises many additional questions. Why was it important to create a democracy in Iraq rather than any other Middle Eastern country? Was creating democracy in Iraq feasible? Would a democratic Iraq actually elect a leader who opposed U.S. interests in the region? If the objective was to promote regional stability to rob terrorists of safe haven, would deposing a secular dictator serve that objective? The purpose here is not to make a judgment about whether the decisions and planning for the invasion of Iraq were good or bad, but to show that a deeper examination of the questions above and a more established theory of victory at the outset of conflict might have proven useful.

Theories of victory also must connect directly to plans for conflict termination and diplomacy. Victory is almost never absolute. Even in the Second World War, when the Allies demanded unconditional victory, many mid-level Nazi leaders were allowed to remain in power under the new regime. Thus, there was some degree of compromise at the termination of conflict. It is also important to realize that an insistence on unconditional surrender can prove counterproductive and result in needless casualties and destruction. Might the Allies have found a way to defeat Germany and remove

Hitler from power by offering options other than unconditional surrender? Leaders must always consider which terms for conflict termination are the most beneficial to overall national interests.

The importance of including war termination and diplomacy in the theory of victory also helps ensure that the means of pursuing strategic objectives do not damage the prospects of the desired diplomatic settlement. For example, if a theory of victory focuses merely on military victory, the means employed in the conflict might inadvertently push the enemy away from the negotiating table, lengthening the conflict and increasing suffering on both sides. Rather, leaders should begin with the desired diplomatic conditions for war termination and work backward to develop the military strategy that will bring about those conditions as quickly as possible.

Finally, it is important to note that a theory of victory can be coherent but still be wrong. For example, after Giulio Douhet wrote his book Command of the Air in 1921, many proponents of air power advanced a theory of victory that insisted that bombing an enemy population could bring direct pressure against an opposing state's political will and force immediate surrender. This theory of victory seemed plausible from a logical perspective but proved flawed in practice.

Despite these complexities associated with formulating a theory of victory, the concept of a theory of victory is quite simple and easy to understand. A theory of victory is a story or narrative that explains in clear, realistic terms how leaders plan to achieve ultimate political objectives. The simple and effective test of a theory of victory is clear articulation and the theory's ability to stand up to questions. If leaders or politicians cannot clearly articulate and defend a theory of victory, the national strategy is most likely flawed.

Prioritized Threats or Goals

Prioritization of threats is a critical element of any strategy. In times of peace, the list of strategic priorities might include various threats to national security. For example, for the United States a hypothetical threat list might look something like:

1. Catastrophic WMD terrorist attack
2. Russian invasion of Europe
3. Non-WMD terrorist attacks on U.S. homeland
4. North Korean invasion of South Korea
5. Chinese expansion in the Pacific

The above list is entire hypothetical and serves only for demonstration purposes. Any list of priorities must account for likelihood and criticality. For example, even if a WMD terrorist attack is less likely than a North Korean invasion of South Korea, the WMD attack carries greater weight because the results are more catastrophic. There is no fixed formula for creating and weighting a prioritized threat list and attempts to make the process overly mathematical frequently cloud effective reasoning.

In a time of war against a single opponent, the prioritized list is both offensive and defensive. It might include different enemy courses of action to consider or counter. It might include various geographical theaters of war. It might also include goals and objectives that will lead to war termination. In either case, in peace or in war, the purpose of the prioritized list is to guide the allocation of resources, particularly planning resources.

While coming up with the right list in the right order is a complex and challenging task, the most frequent mistakes are often simple. To start with, many nations, organizations or military units don't even have such a list. It is important to note that the list must exist in writing. It is not enough to keep a list in mind; the list must physically exist. Next, everyone in the organization must know the list from memory. How can an organization focus priorities when subordinates do not know what those priorities are?

Testing competence in real-world organizations can provide shocking results. Imagine approaching a random worker in a government agency or military unit and asking them to list the top five threats to the nation and the top five priorities of their organization. How many would know the answer? Another interesting test is to ask a higher-level leader if his/her subordinates know the strategic priorities, then testing those subordinates to see if the leader was correct. Frequently, a leader will claim that subordinates know such information when in fact they do not. This is actually a threefold failure. First, the leader failed to disseminate strategic priorities to subordinates. Second, the leader failed to test subordinates to verify their knowledge. Third, the leader made the common and critical mistake of assuming competence without verifying or testing for competence.

It is not enough to simply publish a list of priorities and ensure that everyone memorizes the list. It is also critical to verify that the list actually drives resource allocation and decision making. For example, if a nation forms a list of its top five threats, it might want to allocate 40 percent of its resources to the primary threat, 30 percent to the secondary threat and so forth. Resources include everything from manpower to funds.

Reviewing the process of testing an organization for strategic competence, the first step is to determine if the organization has a prioritized threat list. The next step is to determine if that list is properly disseminated throughout the organization. The final step is to determine whether the list is just a piece of paper or if it actually drives decisions and resource allocation.

When checking for appropriate resource allocation, it is not enough simply to ask a leader how resources are allocated within his/her organization. It is not enough to look at a chart or slide that shows the breakdown of responsibilities. Rather, it is necessary to dig down to ground level and actually verify that claims coincide with reality. Systems often appear functional on the surface but break down under closer scrutiny.

Resource Allocation

The purpose of developing a prioritized threat or goal list is to drive resource allocation and decision making. As shown in the nine elements of strategy diagram, the two are inextricably linked; most of the critical points for effective resource allocation were covered in the previous section. However, two additional factors apply uniquely to resource allocation: flexibility and fungibility.

Even the best threat assessment is only an assessment. Threat assessments can be wrong, and the ongoing process of intelligence collection can prove that initial estimates were misguided. To further complicate the equation, even when initial assessments are accurate, the situation itself can change rapidly and render those assessments obsolete. In order to counter either uncertainty or change, resource allocation must remain flexible.

If a nation is embroiled in a massive counterterrorism and counterinsurgency effort and suddenly must transition to face an existential conventional threat, that nation's survival will depend on how quickly it can shift resource allocation from one set of priorities to another. As with all things, planners should attempt to forecast such eventualities as much as possible. The moment to find out that it will take one year to convert a counterinsurgency-focused military into a conventionally competent military is not when enemy tanks are crossing the border.

Attempting to think ahead not only will help prevent unpleasant surprises but also will help force innovation and effectiveness in key areas. The adage "necessity is the mother of invention" only applies in cases where a necessity was recognized in the first place. For example, in the example above, imagine that analysts determine ahead of time that it will take a year to convert their forces from counterinsurgency focused to conventionally focused. Decision makers might decide that one year is an unacceptable length of time. This brings to the surface a "necessity" that will encourage greater inventive focus on shortening the timeline.

Subordinate leaders and trainers might develop and test new training methods or acquire new technology to cut the transition time from one year to four months. Leaders might start cross-training in both counterinsurgency and conventional operations. Leaders might assign some units to focus on conventional operations and others to focus on counterinsurgency. However, none of these innovations would happen without first understanding and deliberately quantifying the need or gap. It is only when leaders know that it will take one year to transition that they will allocate appropriate resources to shortening that timeline. If they reassure themselves with baseless assumptions that transition will be quick and easy, what imperative will drive innovation?

The second critical element of resource allocation is fungibility. Fungibility derives from the word fungibilis, from fungi, defined by the New Oxford American Dictionary as "able to replace or be replaced by another identical item; mutually interchangeable." The dictionary offers money as an example of something that is fungible; money that is raised for one purpose can also be used for something else. In choosing where to allocate resources, it is important to invest in resources that are as fungible as possible.

For example, many military technological platforms are not very fungible. Many are designed to solve one specific or pressing problem but prove almost useless for other applications. Weapons systems from the Cold War have found limited utility in counterinsurgency operations. Despite leaders' best efforts to advertise the continued relevance of obsolete platforms, it is clear that many weapons have limited applications. For example, highly advanced and expensive stealth technology developed to help aircraft and submarines penetrate advanced sensor networks are of limited use against terrorists or guerrillas armed with improvised explosives, hiding amongst a neutral population.

However, the fungibility sword cuts both ways. The U.S. Army's enormous fleet of Mine Resistant Ambush Protected (MRAP) vehicles will likely prove less useful in a conventional conflict. The same goes for the U.S. overreliance on drones that could not hope to survive against an enemy with any counter-air capability. Figuring out ways to apply the tools of counterinsurgency to conventional war and vice versa is a difficult task that requires a great deal of thinking, training and doctrinal creativity. Perhaps the better option is to attempt to focus on investing in more fungible tools from the outset.

For example, certain intelligence capabilities and sensors could prove equally effective in counterinsurgency and conventional war. Such sensors might help defeat IEDs as well as tools with narrower applications, such as MRAPs. There are many examples of how to allocate resources toward efforts or programs that are more fungible and have multiple applications. Focusing on recruiting and retaining the smartest personnel is universally beneficial. Focusing on technology that streamlines logistics is rarely counterproductive. In summary, when allocating resources, leaders should first ensure that the allocation is flexible enough to adjust if the threat priorities change unexpectedly. Second, when possible, leaders should attempt to invest in fungible resources that provide universal benefits regardless of changes in threat priorities.

The importance of flexibility and fungibility for resource allocation applies particularly to the sort of multiple-decade acquisition programs typical for the U.S. military. For the most advanced weapon systems, the time from inception to fielding is typically decades. Considering how extensively the security environment can change in a decade, it is reasonable to assume that every major weapon system will already be irrelevant or obsolete by the time it rolls off the assembly line. Imagine trying to fight a war with a brand new weapon that was designed to meet the threats of twenty years ago. There are only two solutions to this problem: either create weapons that are fungible enough to prove useful in almost any situation, or let necessity be the mother of invention and find ways to shorten the acquisition timeline, even at the expense of efficiency or quality.

Comparative Capabilities Forecast

This step in the strategic process aligns most closely with the quantitative tradition of military analysis. While recent cultural movements have shunned the Cold War trend of trying to reduce war to an equation, there is indeed a place for equations in the strategic process. However, the depth of calculations must go well beyond mere numerical strength to identify the physical boundaries of possibility on both sides.

Certain inequalities in warfare are either impossible or nearly impossible to counter, particularly in the area of raw materials and industrial and logistical capacity. For example, a nation can have the best tanks in the world manned by the world's most elite crews, but if the nation has only enough fuel for one day of operations, all those advantages come to naught. Certain inescapable, mathematical calculations define the boundaries of possibility within which all other intangible factors must operate. Intangible factors such as leadership, morale, and courage are truly the most important, but they cannot create fuel or bullets from nothing. The intangibles must operate within the bounds of the tangible.

It is interesting to note that while tangible factors are by far the easiest to calculate, they have received very little attention in many historical campaigns. Had Hitler and his staff devoted a concerted effort to precisely calculating the industrial and logistical limitations of the Third Reich, such data might have prevented Germany from embarking on campaigns that were simply mathematical impossibilities. Likewise, had Japan more accurately calculated its industrial capabilities as compared with the United States, it might have forecasted the inevitable result and adopted more desperate approaches earlier in the conflict.

One factor that comes to the surface in examining Germany and Japan is the danger of false reporting or exaggeration, particularly for authoritarian regimes in which punishment comes to the bringer of bad news. In many cases, analysts know the outlook is bleak but are afraid to report accurate findings to superiors for fear of being fired, or worse. The same applies to unit commanders. Commanders who report progress, truthfully or untruthfully, tend to succeed or survive where those who report failure tend to disappear. Essentially, it is in each leader's interest to exaggerate his or her unit's capability and success. This phenomenon can yield inaccuracies that prove fatal in the long run. The only way to counter this problem is to rigidly enforce honest and accurate reporting at every level of command, to verify accuracy with surprise inspections and punish violators.

It is also important for the forecast to be as comprehensive and detailed as possible. For example, a naval force hoping to use air-defense missiles to counter enemy anti-ship missile attacks must know how many anti-ship missiles the enemy has and then exceed that number by a significant margin with its own store of air-defense missiles. However, that only covers the first engagement. Analysis must go further to determine how long it will take to resupply missile stores underway, how long it will take to produce new missiles in factories, and when the raw materials needed to produce missiles will run out. A competent and functional force will keep a running, accurate accounting of these numbers and factor them into planning at all levels.

These planning horizons must exist on the same timeline and remain constantly updated. As much as possible, analysts should also consider how unexpected changes and contingencies will affect the numbers and timeline. For example, estimates for how fast factories can produce missiles should factor in the possibility of enemy efforts to bomb factories and interdict supply lines. Analysts should always build planning numbers and timelines around the worst case scenario, as it is much better to be pleasantly surprised than unpleasantly surprised. If analysts expect that enemy bombing and interdiction will reduce missile stores by half, there will be no unpleasant surprises if the actual reduction is only a quarter.

As with prioritized threat assessment, another critical factor regarding the comparative capabilities forecast is that it actually exists in tangible form. An evaluator must be able to physically see the numbers on a piece of paper or computer screen and check the calculations behind those numbers. The numbers must also find their way to planners, and all plans must operate within the defined boundaries. This might seem obvious, but with two of the most professional militaries in history, the Germans and the Japanese in the Second World War, this was not the case.

Finally, it is important to emphasize that the comparative capabilities forecast is indeed comparative. It is not only important to know one's own industrial and logistical capabilities; it is also critical to know how those capabilities compare with that of various adversaries. Discovery of glaring inequalities can serve as catalysts for innovation and drastic change. For example, identifying a critical shortage of a certain raw material can inspire planning for new trade agreements or industrial innovations.

Strengths and Weaknesses

Analysis of strengths and weaknesses is both the most important and the least quantifiable of the four calculations. In many ways, it is as much a qualitative estimate as it is a quantitative calculation. However, because the strengths and weaknesses assessment is at least partially quantifiable and emerges largely from other numerical data sets, it fits best under the category of calculations.

Analysts should attempt to identify and quantify as many strengths and weaknesses as possible on both sides. It is impossible to predict which imbalance might prove decisive; however, analysts must use their judgment and focus an adequate amount of attention on those imbalances that are deemed most critical.

Choosing which weaknesses or imbalances to focus on is where the act of calculation begins to transition from science to art. Up to this point, most calculations have been fairly straightforward and unambiguous. In analyzing strengths and weaknesses, all of these previous calculations come into play but must then filter through more creative thought processes. For example, if analysts identify a critical material shortage within the enemy industrial system, they must then wargame exactly how to target and exacerbate that shortage before it can truly be considered a weakness. If there is a critical shortage but no practical way to exploit it for positive gain, then it is only a weakness in theory and has no practical value.

The creative process for identifying strengths and weaknesses involves a great deal of wargaming and hypothesizing. Analysts must strive to take the entire picture into account and to anticipate the interactions and outcomes of different events and changes within the competitive equation. For example, some Nazi planners advocated focusing on the Mediterranean theater in 1940 instead of attacking Britain. Superficial historical analysis suggests that this course of action would have been very promising, as the Allies were comparatively weaker in the Mediterranean. However, in examining the whole picture, it becomes clear that if the Germans had focused all their attention on the Mediterranean, the imbalance would not have remained constant; the Allies would have shifted forces to respond to the German move.

The Germans may have increased their chances, but not to the degree suggested by a superficial analysis that ignores the possible redeployment of Allied forces to the Mediterranean theater. Also, if German planes in the Mediterranean were focused on attacking British ships instead of bombing British airfields, how might that have changed the equations? Were the Luftwaffe's anti-ship capabilities adequately developed in terms of training and munitions? Considering the British side, how effective would British fighters have been in the Mediterranean without the benefit of the Chain Home radar system they used in the Battle of Britain?

Analysts must consider all of these types of factors when looking for imbalances.

Given the degree of complexity and ambiguity just described, the best approach to identifying imbalances and targeting enemy weaknesses is to focus on the most obvious and unambiguous cases. This means focusing on areas of proven effectiveness in which the enemy has proven consistently unable to measure up. For example, for the Soviet Union in the Second World War, manpower was an obvious and critical advantage. Any Soviet strategy that did not try to take maximum advantage of manpower and attrition would have been foolish. The Germans, in comparison, needed to try to choose battle conditions that made maximum use of their superior training, mobility and tactical competence.

The principle is simple: Nations must focus primarily on what they are good at and attempt to align those strengths with enemy weaknesses and critical vulnerabilities. While this seems obvious on the surface, it can be difficult to apply in practice. In the interest of improvement or finding a "better way," many nations or forces neglect their strengths and attempt to change their fundamental nature. To offer an analogy, imagine that the most effective hand-to-hand fighting style is the sort of fast-paced, agility-focused martial art practiced by Bruce Lee. In theory, if Bruce Lee's system proves most effective, all fighters should attempt to emulate Bruce Lee in order to achieve maximum effectiveness.

However, is it really practical for a 400-pound sumo wrestler who has spent his entire life training in sumo wrestling to attempt to lose 250 pounds and adopt an entirely new fighting style? Even if sumo is not technically the most effective system, it is probably the most effective for the 400-pound wrestler. The same principle applies to nations and military units. A truly wise leader focuses on how to achieve the best results given the characteristics and constraints of his or her own organization.

For example, recent movements within the U.S. military advocate a reduced focus on technology in favor of building a force more like the German Army in the Second World War that excels in flexibility, maneuver warfare and small unit initiative. While such movements clearly have valid points and might help improve U.S. combat capability, would it ever be practical for the U.S. not to focus on technology, since technology is the area where the U.S. probably has the most commanding lead among world competitors? This is an example of why it is important to focus on strengths rather than try to become something else in pursuit of an ideal outcome. The sumo wrestler probably has a better chance of winning by trying to find a way to capitalize on his size and strength, instead of trying to lose 250 pounds and learn a new fighting style.

Another critical element in analyzing strengths and weaknesses is the effort to create an asymmetric advantage. Even if a force is unable to compete in the most important arena, it might still be able to achieve dominance by focusing on a specific part of the competitive equation. This approach can be particularly effective if that point of focus aligns with an enemy's critical vulnerability. Referencing the functional model, a critical vulnerability is any part of the machine whose suppression or elimination causes the entire system to break down or degrade dramatically. A critical vulnerability is also something that is difficult for the enemy to compensate for or replace.

In the Second World War, Britain's sea lines of communication were a critical vulnerability. Had the Germans managed to cut off the British island completely, the entire British strategic effort would have broken down. Thus, it might have made sense for the Germans to attempt to exploit an asymmetric advantage in their submarine force, focusing a disproportional amount of effort and resources on submarine warfare.

Achieving an asymmetric advantage often involves refusing battle in areas of enemy strength or assuming risk in other domains of competition. For example, Germany might have achieved a truly decisive asymmetric advantage in submarine warfare had they redirected all resources and spending away from less decisive projects such as battleship production or terror bombing.

Focusing on battleship production and bombing were both attempts to beat the British in their areas of greatest strength. The Royal Navy and the RAF Fighter Command were arguably among the most elite forces in Britain. Germany might have refused battle in these areas and instead focused on an area of German strength, the U-boat force. This strength might have proved decisive as it aligned against the inherent critical vulnerabilities of an island nation.

In summary, there is no fixed formula for analyzing strengths and weaknesses. Effectiveness demands a combination of detailed quantitative analysis with insightful qualitative analysis and wargaming. The right course of action for a given force is often suboptimal. It is generally more practical to optimize existing strengths than to try to become something else. In some cases, the best approach might be to focus disproportional effort on securing an asymmetric advantage, even if doing so incurs risk in other areas.

Constraints

"Constraints" is the first element on the "estimates" side of the diagram, and is useful to consider at the outset of the strategic process. Constraints also include requirements or imperatives that limit the realm of strategic possibility, such as unavoidable political or diplomatic concerns that are outside the realm of military planning but have vital implications for national goals.

For example, U.S. military planners are constrained by the laws of war in any operation. When a force has the option to either obey or disobey the laws of war, that will redefine the boundaries of possibility for subsequent strategic concepts. Just as the comparative capabilities forecast defines the "realm of the possible" in mathematical terms, constraints define the realm of the possible in political, diplomatic and strategic terms.

There are many examples of how constraints can affect planning. When facing a nuclear opponent, an imperative to prevent conflict escalation into the nuclear realm may constrain action. This might result a conscious effort to limit the application of combat power to avoid putting the enemy in a "desperate" position where nuclear release might seem a viable option. Constraints might also include avoidance of casualties because of domestic political factors. For instance, U.S. air operations in the Balkans in the 1990s had to factor casualty avoidance heavily into operational planning.

These are only a few examples of how constraints can affect strategic options. A final point to remember is that many types of constraints, particularly political constraints, cannot be simply wished away or used as an excuse for ineffectiveness. Military leaders often make statements about what they could do if only the political constraints would go away. While it is acceptable for military planners to voice such concerns, and doing so might influence political perspectives, it is unrealistic to expect political constraints to go away entirely. Rather, it is the planner's duty to either work around the political constraints or to have the courage to declare that a military option is unfeasible in the existing political environment.

Enemy Perspective

Analyzing the enemy perspective is a uniquely important mental exercise. It is connected with the more quantitative efforts of comparative capabilities assessment and strengths and weaknesses assessment, and necessary for the strategic planning process. What sets this step apart from other steps is that it focuses less on the actual reality of the competitive equation and more on the perception of the enemy force itself. It is possible to conduct an insightful analysis of both sides and still miss critical factors that influence enemy capability and action. Much of the effort in enemy perspective analysis seeks to find the missing pieces of the enemy's half of the equation, so far overlooked by other analytical efforts. These missing pieces often will be more related to intangible, irrational or human factors.

It is quite tempting to view the enemy as perfectly rational beings operating in a flawless system. An even more dangerous error is "mirror imaging," or assuming the enemy thinks in the same way as friendly forces do. It is only by stepping into the enemy's shoes and trying to see through the enemy's eyes that such fallacies become clear. The effort is not to see the world accurately but rather to see the world the way the enemy sees it, complete with bias, cultural conditioning, irrationality, political corruption and stupidity. Failing to include these elements in the planning process runs the risk of grossly misrepresenting the true nature of the strategic equation.

Contingencies

As noted in the introduction, it is always critical to consider contingencies at every level. This point will emerge over and over, as it relates to nearly every aspect of military operations and planning. For any given strategic plan, it is vital to consider at least one contingency: the worst-case scenario. For the French in 1940, the worst-case scenario was a German invasion in the south through the Ardennes Forest. The French should have had a contingency plan for dealing with this possibility.

There are two critical points to consider when identifying the worst-case scenario and developing contingency plans to deal with it. First, it is difficult to know what the worst-case scenario (referred to by the U.S. military as the "enemy's most dangerous course of action" or MDCOA) without knowing the specifics of the friendly strategy or course of action. For instance, a German attack in the south was only the most dangerous because the French had decided to focus their defenses in the north. Had the French decided to focus their defenses in the south, the opposite German course of action may have proved the most dangerous.

The second factor to consider is that a contingency plan is not an entirely different plan with a different set of starting conditions. A contingency plan is a way to adjust a primary plan on the fly to deal with unexpected change. For the French in 1940, a sample contingency plan would not have been to reposition all forces at the outset to counter a southern attack, as the French had already determined to focus on stopping an attack in the north. Thus, a contingency plan would have built on the fixed initial conditions of a northern deployment and would explain how such a force would adjust midstride to counter a southern attack.

While it is necessary to form at least one contingency plan to deal with the enemy's most dangerous course of action, it is advisable to plan for additional contingencies given adequate time and resources. Detailed planning for multiple contingencies is often discouraged by the age-old principle that it is impossible to plan for everything. In reality, this principle applies more to physical resources than to planning resources. Within the realm of practicality, planners should plan for as many contingencies as time and resources will allow.

Multiple contingency plans do not have to be detailed and should not detract from the momentum of the main planning effort. The utility of multiple contingency plans truly comes into play in situations where large bureaucracies and staffs have an extended planning cycle with no time constraints. Given these conditions, it might make sense to assign hundreds of planners and analysts to develop hundreds of contingency plans and file them away, only pulling them out in the event that the contingency actually materializes.

Even if this mass of contingency plans was superficial and each plan only involved a few days' work by a single analyst, a small head start might prove decisive in responding to what would otherwise be a complete surprise. If the analyst who predicted the contingency was still available, the analyst might be called to act as an advisor to high-level decision makers, as the given analyst would have spent more time thinking about this particular set of events than anyone else in the country.

This is just one example of how to apply multiple contingency plans in a useful way. The main reason "more is better" when it comes to contingency planning is due to the overwhelming and destabilizing effects of complete surprise in warfare. When a force achieves complete surprise, they achieve not only an advantage in space and time but also gain disproportional benefits from disorienting the adversary. According to fighter pilot and military theorist John Boyd, the second step in his Observe-Orient-Decide-Act (OODA) loop is the most critical. A surprised force becomes disoriented and must reorient itself to the new, unexpected reality. Having at least a superficial contingency plan in place greatly reduces this disorientation effect.

In this way, contingency plans relate to the U.S. Army's concept of a "battle drill." Generally, the purpose of a battle drill is primarily to buy the tactical leader time to make a better tactical decision. The battle drill provides an acceptable, immediately executable response that will likely prove better than doing nothing at all. While the automated process is running, the leader has time to observe the specific situation and make adjustments as needed. Having contingency plans in place helps leaders avoid the disorienting shock and paralysis that comes from total surprise.

Outcomes

It is critically important for planners to consider the outcomes of any strategy. Outcomes are different from end states or objectives in that outcomes encompass both intended and unintended consequences. For example, victory in the First World War eventually led to the Second World War. It would have been difficult but possible for planners and analysts to predict this causal chain of events. Victory in the First World War was extremely costly, necessitating imposition of steep reparations payments on Germany, which built resentment and desperation within the German populace. It is impossible to predict the future, but analysts must at least do their best to anticipate any unintended outcomes--particularly negative outcomes--that might guide alterations to the planning process.

Considering outcomes is particularly important in low-intensity conflict where such outcomes often form a key part of the deliberate objectives of terrorist or insurgent forces. The French military in Algeria was so focused on winning a tactical victory against the Algerian FLN (National Liberation Front) that they failed to consider the unintended negative impact that brutality and torture would have on world opinion and political resolve. It is critical to attempt to predict such outcomes to avoid strategic or political failure.

Training Strategists: Strategic Science vs. Strategic Genius

When scholars suggest that the art of strategy cannot be taught or quantified, they are most likely referring to the less tangible elements of strategic genius that are often the most essential or decisive ingredient for victory. There is indeed no checklist or fixed curriculum that can guarantee strategic success or competence. However, the concept of controlling the controllables in order to free up maximum bandwidth for more ambiguous problems applies at the strategic level as well as every other level of warfare.

The nine elements of strategy discussed this far represent the more controllable aspects of the strategic equation. Many critical strategic failures in history are not the result of lack of genius but rather the absence of one or more of the nine outlined elements. Such failures could realistically have been avoided simply through internalizing and applying the nine elements. This realization makes the prospect of improving strategy or training strategists seem less daunting. Even if it is not possible to train a strategic genius, it is at least possible to train someone to avoid the strategic mistakes that proved to be the primary cause of failure in a majority of historical case studies.

Training in these more empirical and mechanical elements of strategy is no different from any other kind of training. High-level politicians and generals might consider it beneath them to engage in frequent practice or drills, but such training evolutions are the only way to improve performance when the crisis comes. When high-level leaders are performing tasks associated with strategic planning and crisis response, it is often the first time any of them have performed such tasks, though it might have been possible to predict and practice these tasks beforehand. How is it realistic to expect people to do something well if they have never done it before? It would be considered inexcusable if even the lowest ranking soldier in an army proved incapable of firing a weapon because he/she had not been afforded the opportunity to practice. Should the same standard not apply to national leaders?

The actual format of strategic practice or drill would be fairly straightforward and remain within the scope of the nine elements of strategy discussed this far. Leaders, strategists and the analysts serving under them should periodically run through the process of allocating resources, forecasting capabilities, analyzing strengths and weaknesses, forming contingencies, and predicting outcomes. While practicing only once or twice is better than no practice at all, real improvement only comes with multiple repetitions under varying conditions.

There are countless administrative and technical tasks associated with strategic planning. Therefore, practice must not be limited to the general actions of higher-level leaders but must extend down to the specific administrative and technical actions of staff in support of higher-level activities. Practicing and streamlining bureaucratic processes, establishing dependable channels for interagency coordination, and developing and disseminating standard operating procedures for accomplishing mundane tasks quickly and effectively all contribute to strategic success, and demand practice and refinement.

The less tangible aspects of the strategic art are difficult to quantify, teach or practice. As discussed, focusing on tangibles or controllable factors can help set the conditions under which the intangibles arts can flourish by freeing up time and mental bandwidth. However, such efforts can only create space or opportunity and cannot guarantee creative brilliance.

While there is no formula for fostering strategic genius, the more brilliant strategic minds generally have a strong grasp of numerous historical case studies and/or have had many opportunities to practice strategy in real life. Greater amounts of experience, first- or secondhand, helps develop a capacity for pattern recognition that can at the very least enhance strategic brilliance, if not help create it. The best way to pursue strategic mastery is immersion in historical case studies, wargames and exercises.

Defense

The fundamental techniques and skills associated with defense are simple and intuitive. However, in reality, many military units fail to achieve even marginal results in defensive performance. Running through the fundamentals of defensive operations and comparing them to actual practice in real operations will highlight the importance of these fundamentals while also showing how easy they are to overlook.

Building on the previous discussion of how best to organize learning topics, defensive operations are a natural point of departure. Many theories differentiate offense from defense, sometimes labeling them as opposites or two halves of a whole. This fundamental misunderstanding of the nature of defense and offense is one of the root causes for poor combat performance.

Defense and offense are not opposites nor are they two halves of a whole. Offensive operations must have a clear, positive objective. They must be planned, and have a start point and a defined end state. Defensive operations never stop; they encompass every other type of operation, including offensive operations. The reason for this is the inevitable uncertainty of the battlefield. Since forces can never feel entirely secure, they must always be prepared to defend themselves against the unexpected.

When planning an offensive operation, the assembly areas where that planning takes place must be defended from enemy attack and observation. Even advancing forces must defend themselves against enemy counterattack. When units are refitting on home soil, apparently safe from immediate threat, they still must defend themselves to some degree or potentially plan to deploy as part of a reserve force to support defensive operations elsewhere. Defensive readiness levels go up and down, but the process of defensive operations never stops. Thus, just as the strategic level of war encompasses the operational and tactical levels, defensive operations encompass all other forms of operations.

Defense Fundamentals

Strategic and Operational Threat Assessment

Defensive planning begins with the strategic threat assessment we have discussed. Strategic decision makers complete a prioritized threat list and disseminate that list down to subordinate units to form the basis for defensive planning. Subordinate units may cross talk with strategic planners to adjust defensive priorities based on specific regional or operational circumstances. For example, if strategic decision makers determine that terrorism is the highest-priority threat for the nation, forces stationed in South Korea still might want to focus most of their attention on the North Korean threat. Thus, strategic threat priorities serve only as a guide for developing an operational threat assessment specific to a unit's given region or situation.

As a unit develops its operational threat assessment, it must evaluate threats in terms of both gravity and likelihood. Military forces have developed many methods of doing this, including threat matrices and other mathematical models. For example, in a threat matrix, planners assign each threat a value of 1-5 for gravity and a value of 1-5 for likelihood. Planners can add additional criteria to the matrix such as force strength, training, morale etc. Finally, planners can assign weights to each of these criteria if they deem some criteria are more critical than others. The resulting numbers allow planners to use mathematical calculations to determine the priority of threats.

It is critical to understand, however, that some of these systems can be ineffective and misleading. They were developed to give the illusion of quantitative analysis, when in reality the analysis is still qualitative, as the numbers assigned to threats are ultimately subjective and based on human thinking rather than measurable data. Thus, the further a system takes planners away from actually using their brains and focusing on good qualitative analysis, the less effective that system will be. It can still be helpful to use some matrices or calculations to assist the analytical process, but these systems must be essentially simple and not detract from natural human thinking and common sense.

The final product will list all threats in order of priority. Once again, as each threat is weighed in terms of gravity and likelihood, even threats that are unlikely to occur might earn a high priority if their results are potentially catastrophic. For example, even if the threat of a domestic nuclear terrorist attack is unlikely, it may still earn a top priority over a potentially more likely threat of a Chinese attack on Taiwan. Though it may be determined highly likely that the Chinese will attack Taiwan, the result of such an attack would not be as grave for U.S. national security as a nuclear attack on the homeland. Using this kind of judgment and analysis, planners must do their best to rank all threats in order of priority.

Enemy Courses of Action and Contingency Planning

Once a unit has completed the operational threat assessment, the next step is to wargame specific contingencies of how each threat could play out in real life. This starts the process of forming a matrix of contingency plans that extends down the chain of command to the lowest level units. For example, in the 1980s, if planners had anticipated that an Iraqi invasion of Kuwait was a top priority threat in the Middle East, the next question would have been to determine how such an attack would play out. There would likely be several possibilities or enemy courses of action.

It is unrealistic to attempt to consider every possible enemy course of action or to try to anticipate enemy courses of action down to the smallest detail. When developing enemy courses of action, the main focus should be to identify in general terms the most likely enemy course of action and then consider the worst case scenario, or the enemy's most dangerous course of action. Referring to the previous discussion of French defensive planning in 1940, the French did a good job selecting what they considered to be the enemy's most likely course of action, an attack in the north through Belgium.

However, the French could have at least considered one alternate course of action, a surprise attack through the Ardennes Forest. Though this course of action seemed unlikely and was risky for the Germans, the French should have considered it because it was the one move that had the potential of completely unhinging the French defense and causing catastrophic defeat. In U.S. Army planning terms, an attack through the Ardennes was the enemy's most dangerous course of action.

Many modern military schools teach planners to develop at minimum two enemy courses of action: the most likely course of action (MLCOA) and the most dangerous course of action (MDCOA). However, some schools fail to fully understand the nature and relationship of these two courses of action. In many cases, planners develop both the enemy's most likely course of action and the enemy's most dangerous course of action first, then go on to develop friendly courses of action. In these cases, the most dangerous course of action often simply involves a larger or more aggressive enemy action. Thus, the way planners typically plan follows the steps below:

1. Develop the enemy's most likely course of action
2. Develop the enemy's most dangerous course of action
3. Develop friendly courses of action to counter the enemy

The above steps are out of order. The correct way to plan is first to develop the enemy's most likely course of action, then to develop the friendly course of action to counter that most likely course of action. Only then is it possible to develop the enemy's most dangerous course of action. The most dangerous course of action is not only "bigger" but also takes advantage of the weaknesses in the friendly course of action. Thus it is impossible to know the enemy's most dangerous course of action without first knowing the friendly course of action.

When planners have developed the enemy's most dangerous course of action, they return and develop at least one contingency plan to counter that most dangerous course of action. The contingency plan is not an entirely different plan but rather a way to adjust the existing plan midstride in the event that the enemy deviates from their most likely course of action. If wargaming shows that transitioning between the main plan and the contingency plan is difficult or impossible, planners might need to go back and adjust the main plan to allow for easier transition to the contingency plan.

In the France 1940 example, the French determined that the German's most likely course of action was to attack in the north, and they proceeded to develop a defensive plan to counter this most likely course of action. The French did identify the most dangerous course of action but failed to develop a contingency plan to deal with it. For the French, a contingency plan would not have called for deploying forces in the south but would rather have explained how forces positioned to defend in the north could reposition on the fly to counter an unexpected southern attack. If the French had determined that distances or terrain made it impossible to redeploy forces to the south quickly enough to respond to a southern attack, French planners might have had to adjust the main plan, making it more balanced or flexible. The proper steps for defensive planning are:

1. Develop the enemy's most likely course of action.
2. Develop friendly plan to counter the enemy's most likely course of action.
3. Develop the enemy's most dangerous course of action (to exploit the weaknesses of the plan developed in step 2).
4. Develop friendly contingency plans to counter the enemy's most dangerous course of action.
5. Adjust the main plan as needed to allow for effective transition between the main plan and the contingency plan.

Cyclical Interplay between Operations and Intelligence

The process described above for planning and contingency planning is inseparable from the intelligence process. While each of the previous five steps are taking place, there is a simultaneous, asynchronous and cyclical interplay of planning and intelligence. Note that in order to effectively explain the interplay between intelligence and planning, some references to offensive operations will be needed. The cyclical interplay of planning and intelligence is sometimes overlooked in modern military schools.

Some planning techniques and methodologies suggest that a plan can be effectively assembled using only the intelligence initially available at the start of the planning process. Consequently, in the worst cases, planners collect every bit of intelligence they have that might be useful for an operation, consider that intelligence as "fact," and proceed to develop a highly complex, detailed plan over an extended planning interval. Planners who correctly apply the army's Military Decision-Making Process (MDMP) at least realize that all necessary intelligence might not be available at the start of an operation.

MDMP calls for identifying information gaps, then developing intelligence collection requirements and corresponding intelligence collection plans to fill those gaps. For example, planners might realize they know almost nothing about the composition of forces defending a given river. The planning process would identify information gaps and then specific detailed intelligence collection requirements, such as "How large a force is defending the river? How are forces arrayed? What kind of weapons do they have?" The planning process would then assign specific intelligence or reconnaissance assets to collect that information. For example, planners might immediately call for a reconnaissance aircraft to fly over the river and take pictures to collect the specified information. Such pictures would be necessary to inform and drive the ongoing planning process.

However, because the MDMP process places intelligence and reconnaissance planning early in the planning process, it has a tendency to become a "one-time thing" as opposed to an ongoing interplay. This misses the critical point that intelligence rapidly goes stale. If an aircraft flies over the river and collects accurate information but it is another eight hours before the plan is complete, might the intelligence used to formulate the plan already be obsolete by the time the plan is ready to execute?

The only way to solve this problem is to view intelligence not as a step in the planning process but rather as part of a never-ending cycle between intelligence and operations that must spin faster and faster in order to outpace the enemy's reaction time. When viewed in this way, the importance of aggressive, fluid and free-flowing operations becomes all the more apparent. For example, many planners might plan an attack as follows:

1. Establish defensive posture
2. Begin planning

3. Identify information gaps
4. Plan and execute reconnaissance to fill information gaps
5. Complete the plan
6. Execute the plan

Such a rigid approach does not consider the enemy as a living, thinking opponent bent on subverting every friendly move. A more aggressive, fluid and free-flowing plan might look like this:

1. Immediately attack into known areas of enemy weakness to fight for intelligence and to spoil the enemy's decision-making process by keeping them off balance
2. While attacking, use the information flow from the front to plan a larger-scale attack
3. Identify information gaps
4. Plan and execute reconnaissance to fill information gaps; maintain persistent surveillance on enemy movements whenever possible
5. Attempt to identify enemy intentions and execute feints or deception plans to draw the enemy into a position of vulnerability
6. Attack or screen enemy reconnaissance capabilities to prevent them from identifying the real friendly course of action
7. Complete the plan
8. Execute the plan

The more aggressive approach outlined above recognizes the urgency created by the constant fluctuation and inevitable uncertainty of battlefield conditions. As friendly forces are collecting intelligence and developing a plan, the enemy is also collecting intelligence and developing their own plan to counter the friendly plan. At any point during the competitive planning process, either side can stage a spoiling attack to throw off the opposing planning cycle or disrupt opposing preparations. Either side might also use deception to cause opposing planners to stumble into a trap, or to waste time and planning resources to counter an imaginary contingency. Whichever side is able to do all these things more effectively, dynamically and quickly will outpace the opposing decision cycle.

INTELLIGENCE PLANNING AND INDICATORS

Developing indicators that point to specific enemy courses of action is critical for defensive planning. Returning to the discussion of the enemy's most likely and most dangerous courses of action, how can planners identify which course of action the enemy is choosing as early as possible? Using the France 1940 example, the French might have developed an intelligence collection plan that focused on aerial reconnaissance of key assembly areas, road junctions or river crossings leading to German avenues of approach through the Ardennes Forest. In U.S. Army planning terms, the French would have established NAIs (Named Areas of Interest) at these points and provided specific collection requirements for each NAI.

It is important to provide specific collection requirements so the collectors know exactly what to look for. It is also necessary to estimate what criteria would suggest that the enemy has chosen the most dangerous course of action. For example, a certain size of unit moving through the Ardennes Forest could have indicated that the Germans were attacking in the south. Alternately, the presence of certain elite German units in the south would also suggest that the German main effort was in the south. In reality, the French overlooked all of these considerations. French reconnaissance planes actually did see many German headlights along Ardennes roads, but because the planners and pilots had not identified specific NAIs and developed specific indicators or collection requirements, the information did not help the French take the appropriate actions.[28]

Thus, for any defensive plan, it is essential to tie each enemy course of action to a series of NAIs, each with specific collection requirements and indicators. This will serve as a baseline for reading enemy actions and implementing contingencies accordingly. This process cannot be robotic because a clever enemy will execute feints with the express purpose of "tripping" the execution criteria for friendly contingency plans. Thus, NAIs and indicators serve only as guidelines for decision making.

Planning for the Reserve

Adjusting a plan to meet the requirements of various contingencies frequently involves adjusting the size and location of the reserve. A reserve force is kept in the rear or in a location that makes it difficult for the enemy to destroy them or pin them down. The reserve typically stands ready to respond to any of the enemy course of actions outlined in the friendly plan. The reserve also gives the friendly commander flexibility to deal with unexpected developments. In the case of France in 1940, the French might have placed a reserve force in position to reinforce either the north or south, based on the enemy course of action to which intelligence indicators were pointing.

In general, the greater the level of uncertainty in an operation, the larger the reserve should be. In some cases, it might be necessary to have multiple reserve forces. The size and location of the reserve can change at any time as new intelligence flows in and the plan solidifies. For example, if at the start of the planning process there is a very high level of uncertainty, the reserve force might be very large. If, however, the planning process reveals new information about enemy forces, portions of the reserve can deploy to reinforce defensive positions accordingly, leaving a smaller reserve to deal with the unexpected.

Reserves also typically exist on different levels. For example, a company commander might establish a reserve squad or reserve platoon that he/she can deploy as needed in support of company-level operations. However, there might also be a battalion reserve and a brigade reserve that can only be deployed with the consent of higher commanders. Leaders at each level must establish plans for incorporating any one of these reserve elements into the defense. This is particularly important for coordinating the arrival and integration of reserve elements outside a unit's immediate chain of command.

For example, what if a company is being overrun and the battalion commander decides to send the battalion reserve platoon to reinforce? That reserve cannot just arrive haphazardly without a prior plan for integrating into the existing defense. Rather, the company commander on the ground must have preplanned locations and fighting positions for the battalion reserve platoon to assume when it arrives. Ideally, the company commander already will have talked with the leader of the reserve forces and pre-established signals, linkup procedures and control measures to facilitate maximum speed, safety and effectiveness. If prior coordination is not possible, a commander should have designated personnel who are preassigned to act as guides for incoming reinforcements, guiding them to the right positions and providing the information they need to integrate effectively into the defensive plan.

The commander on the ground must also know the "time string" for each level of reinforcement. For example, it may take 10 minutes for the battalion reserve to arrive but 30 minutes for the brigade reserve to arrive. Knowing this time string will allow the company commander to plan accordingly and to estimate things like how much ammunition will be needed to hold out long enough for reinforcements to arrive. Planning for the reserves also applies to other support assets such as air support or artillery.

Indicators and Alert Levels

Intelligence collection and indicators also inform alert levels. Identifying and rehearsing alert levels is critical to any defensive plan, as a unit cannot be on 100 percent alert indefinitely. Human beings need to sleep, eat and conduct countless other activities in order to sustain life and stay sharp. A unit that is on maximum alert all the time will be less prepared than a unit that has taken advantage of opportunities to rest and refit when appropriate.

Alert level must be tied to two things: posture and response time. Posture includes everything from how many troops are manning defenses, what they are wearing, how many vehicles have their engines running, and whether or not bullets are chambered in weapons. Each posture must also be connected with specific response time intervals indicating how long it will take to either deploy or to reach the next level of readiness. Units will typically assign code words, numbers or colors to various stages of alert.

For example, imagine an infantry platoon is designated as the battalion reserve in a counterinsurgency operation. That means that the platoon must remain on call at all times to come to the aid of other units in the battalion that might be in trouble. The platoon leader might identify four levels of alert; using army terminology, they might be labeled readiness condition (REDCON) 1-4. Below is a hypothetical example of what each REDCON level might mean.

REDCON	POSTURE	RESPONSE TIME
1	All troops sitting in running vehicles, ready to go	1 minute
2	Troops fully dressed in combat gear, confined to barracks, can use the bathroom but not eat, sleep or shower	5 minutes
3	Troops fully dressed with boots on but combat gear can be staged nearby, troops not confined to barracks, troops can eat and sleep but not shower	10 minutes
4	Troops can wear whatever they want and can eat, sleep or shower	20 minutes

It is important to note that response times are not just assumed to be accurate based on the posture directives. Units must repeatedly rehearse going from one alert level to another to ensure they can meet the response times in a real combat situation. It is also important to realize that while tactical examples make alert levels easy to conceptualize, the exact same concepts apply at every level of warfare. The same principles apply to ensuring a division or rapid deployment force can cross the ocean in time to support a crumbling theater-level defense.

Alert levels apply both to forces in defensive positions and forces allocated as reserve. As stated, commanders must know the time string for the arrival of various reserve elements. Unfortunately, this number is not fixed but is instead tied to alert levels. A reserve's alert level determines how long it will take the reserve to arrive at the reinforcement site. The total response time for a reserve is equal to the transit time plus the response time for the given alert level. So, based on the above chart, if battalion planners know that an operation will take place 20 minutes away from where the reserve location and that the reserve is at REDCON 3, the total response time to the battle area will be 30 minutes.

Wargaming and Backward Planning

The most important thing to consider about response times and alert levels is how to use wargaming and backward planning to ensure there are no unpleasant surprises in a real combat situation. Many units form half-baked plans without performing adequate rehearsals, wargames and time/distance calculations to determine how events could actually play out on the battlefield. Essentially, if the reserve does not arrive in time, it may not be bad luck but rather a sign of dysfunction and incompetent planning.

A common example of this sort of problem relates to the placement of security cameras or sensors. For example, imagine a security force thinks that smugglers are transporting explosives across a river and landing at a particular point on the near bank. The security force sets up a sensor or camera to watch the suspected landing site. A few days later, the unit sees exactly what it expected to see; smugglers land in a boat and begin unloading heavy objects from the boat into a truck. Everyone watching the feed is very excited at first, until they realize they failed to conduct the proper backward planning to actually do anything about what they see on the screen. By the time forces arrive, the smugglers are long gone.

The correct way to solve such a problem involves estimating how long it will take for smugglers to transfer explosives from a boat to a vehicle. If the answer is 5 minutes, then the unit must have a response force able to be on-site in 5 minutes. If this response time is unfeasible, the unit must find other ways to achieve success. For example, maybe there is only one road leading away from the landing site and it runs for five miles before it hits a fork or intersection. In this case, friendly forces might have ten minutes from initial alert to reach the fork in the road.

Whatever planners come up with, the times must add up. The demands of response time dictate the alert levels or the positioning of units. Again, it is critical for commanders to determine all of this before the action starts. If a theater-level defense can only hold out for seven days before it needs reinforcements, strategic planners must find a way to get reinforcements on-site within seven days. This might mean forward-deploying units to advanced bases or using air transport.

There can also be phased reinforcement plans. For example, maybe a company on its own can hold out for ten minutes. That means the battalion reserve must be no more than 10 minutes away. If a company plus the battalion reserve can only hold out for 30 minutes, then the brigade reserve must be no more than 30 minutes away. This type of time-phased planning is particularly important for larger scale operations.

Counterattack

Counterattack is one of the most effective techniques at all levels of warfare. The essence of a counterattack is that it strikes the enemy when they are irrevocably committed or exposed. Again, deception can be useful in setting up a counterattack, drawing the enemy down the path of least resistance only to surprise them when they least expect it.

Counterattacks can also be effective when the enemy reaches a "culminating point." This is particularly true in larger scale operations. Determining the enemy's culminating point requires accurate intelligence about enemy sustainment and logistics capabilities. No advance can maintain momentum indefinitely, and good defensive planners can time a counterattack to hit the enemy just as they run out of steam.

The details of how to conduct a counterattack do not belong with instructions on defensive operations but rather fall under the category of offensive operations. A counterattack is very similar to a deliberate attack except that the reconnaissance phase is largely completed merely through the act of defense. Fighting the defensive battle reveals where most of the enemy forces are and allows the attack planners to choose the ideal time and place to strike.

Intelligence

This chapter on intelligence and the next chapter on planning provide critical points necessary for understanding the following chapter on conducting offensive operations. Intelligence and planning are also relevant to the previous chapters on defense and strategy, but to put chapters on intelligence and planning before those on strategy and defense would be putting the cart before the horse. It is difficult to conduct any intelligence or planning activities without first establishing a strategic context in which to operate. It is also difficult to conduct intelligence or planning without first establishing security and a defensive posture.

Accordingly, the sequence of chapters follows the order that practitioners should follow when approaching the problem of how to create or refine a military or security force. The first step is to establish an overall strategy, at minimum a tentative strategy to provide some context for further action. The next or simultaneous step is to hastily establish a defensive posture to secure the force as it exists and to buy time for further planning and refinement. Once the force is reasonably secure in defensive positions, the next step is to venture out and learn more about the situation, enemy, and environment through intelligence. This order applies to all levels of military operations from strategic to tactical.

Interaction of Intelligence and Operations

We have defined intelligence as a never-ending process that continually interacts with the operations process. When planning for any operation, there are inevitably information gaps to fill before it is possible to complete the plan. To make matters worse, even if intelligence collection and analysis fill these information gaps, planners can rarely be certain that intelligence is accurate. Therefore, planners must complete plans with incomplete information. Additionally, the situation is likely to change from one minute to the next, rendering current intelligence reports useless. This degree of uncertainty and change emphasizes the need for intelligence to be a never-ending process.

This process involves the interaction of intelligence and operations. Intelligence drives operations, but operations subsequently create changes in the situation that call for updating the intelligence picture. An offensive move might cause the enemy to mobilize reserve forces or adjust positions on the battlefield. Intelligence must capture these events and keep the picture constantly up to date. Operations also bring new information gaps to the surface that increase the intelligence burden. Operations might inadvertently answer intelligence requirements or render outstanding requirements moot, demanding a reshuffling of intelligence requirements and priorities. Intelligence and operations interact on every level in countless ways.

The Intelligence Cycle

Apart from constantly interacting with the flow of operations, intelligence itself cycles through a logical sequence. While there are several different versions of the intelligence cycle, they all follow a general sequence of five steps: requirements, tasking, collection, analysis and dissemination.

The cycle begins with requirements, and requirements emerge from the gaps discovered by the planning process. An intelligence requirement is not valid or necessary unless it helps someone make a decision or complete a plan. Intelligence requirements must be ranked in order of priority to help taskers and collectors understand which requirements are the most urgent and important.

The next step is tasking. Once a requirement is established and assigned a level of priority, leaders must determine how best to collect the needed intelligence given the collection assets available. In some cases, the best way to collect the intelligence might be an aerial reconnaissance platform; in other cases, only a human source will be able to collect the needed intelligence. There might also be situations where the ideal collection asset is not available and leaders must settle for a suboptimal solution.

After tasking a specific collection asset to collect the intelligence, that asset must go out and conduct the collection operation. In some cases, such a reconnaissance or surveillance operation is a complex operation in itself, requiring its own detailed process of pre-mission analysis and planning. Thus, the plan to execute a reconnaissance mission in support of a larger plan will probably require its own plan-within-a-plan, further complicating the equation.

When the collection mission is complete, the raw intelligence then requires analysis and processing to make it understandable and useful for decision makers. Analysis might include translating communications intercepts, interpreting reconnaissance photographs, or comparing intelligence from a variety of sources to ensure accuracy. All of these actions demand the specialized skills of experienced intelligence analysts and are generally beyond the capacity of the operations planning team. This underscores the importance of not passing raw intelligence to planners, in order to avoid misinterpretations.

The analyzed intelligence must then be disseminated back to the planners and decision makers who requested it in the first place. The intelligence might also prove useful to other planners and leaders who did not explicitly request the intelligence. However, there are two critical challenges associated with intelligence dissemination that make it a nuanced art. The first challenge is to ensure that every decision maker gets the information he/she needs but is not overwhelmed with irrelevant noise that obscures the most critical information.

The second challenge relates to operational security and compartmentalization. Some intelligence cannot be shared freely because it runs the risk of compromising sensitive sources and methods. These considerations must also factor into the decision of which information to pass to which consumer. While these problems might appear daunting on the surface, there are a series of principles and methods that can greatly improve the effectiveness of the intelligence cycle.

Mechanics of the Intelligence System

Ensuring competence and functionality in the realm of intelligence relates less to theory and more to the mundane details of real-world practice. The majority of intelligence mistakes emerge from simple oversights, laziness, or faulty administrative procedures. Intelligence is a game of details; thus, the mechanical process of capturing and filtering those details is paramount. Most intelligence operations revolve around two products: a requirements list and a common operating picture. While specific techniques may differ in various countries or organizations, the core methods remain generally constant.

Requirements List

One of the most challenging aspects of the intelligence process is keeping track of the numerous intelligence requirements across all units and at all levels of command. The only effective way to do this is for every unit to maintain a constantly updated list of all the outstanding intelligence requirements significant to that unit. As the planning and operations process progresses, intelligence requirements will emerge. The moment planners identify a new requirement, they must pass the requirement to the intelligence section, which will then add it to the running requirements list. The requirements list must at minimum include the following:

1. **Prioritization:** Each requirement must be ranked in order of priority.

2. **Time of Posting:** The time the requirement was first posted.

3. **Time Window for Collection/Dissemination:** Is there a specific time window in which the intelligence must be collected or disseminated? In some cases it is better to collect intelligence later, as in the case of an aerial flyover of enemy positions prior to an attack. If such a flyover took place a week before the attack, the images might prove outdated. In other cases, intelligence needs to be collected sooner because there might be a point where a piece of intelligence is no longer useful or relevant.

4. **Requesting Unit(s) or Intelligence Consumer:** This tells the collectors or analysts where to send the results when the intelligence product is complete.

5. **Collection Asset or Intelligence Provider:** This specifies which unit or asset is responsible for collecting or providing the intelligence. In some cases this might be a collection asset; in other cases it might be a higher-level headquarters. For example, in some cases a unit will not task out an intelligence requirement directly to an asset but will rather pass the requirement to a higher-level intelligence section. That section might already have the information, they might need to task their own assets

to collect it, or they might pass the requirement down to subordinate units that might have the information.

6. **Current Status and Expected Time of Delivery:** This section is filled out by the provider, to keep the consumer informed on the status of the request. For example, if the consumer asks for aerial reconnaissance photos and the reconnaissance unit knows they will not be able to get the photos back and analyzed for another 24 hours, they will post the appropriate date and time under the status block of the requirements list. This will help planners know when to expect certain pieces of intelligence so they can request expedited service if needed and do not waste time waiting for intelligence to arrive.

Once again, it is the responsibility of each individual unit to maintain its own requirements list. Maintaining updated lists requires a great deal of lateral and vertical communication. For example, in order for an intelligence provider to "fill in" the status of a current requirement, it will most likely need to have a conversation with the consumer to synchronize requirements lists. Any time a unit changes its requirements list, it must look at all the consumers or providers connected to that requirement and disseminate the change to each of them.

There are automated or digital ways of synchronizing requirements lists, but these frequently prove problematic, for several reasons. First, they are often poorly designed, ineffective, or not user friendly. Second, these methods often create inaccurate reports by forcing them to conform to a rigid format or input process. Third, they discourage real-time verbal dialogue between units and levels of command, which is possibly one of the most critical ingredients for success. Finally, should an enemy find a way to disable a force's electronic systems, that force might prove unable to operate in the "old-fashioned way" and the apparent advantage of technology might transform into a critical and exploitable vulnerability. Consequently, while technology is useful, it can be problematic.

Requirements can pass from unit to unit both laterally and vertically, forming a complex web of interaction. A battalion might send requirements up to the brigade at the same time the brigade is sending different requirements down to the battalion. Sometimes the tasking chain for a requirement can be very long. For example, a battalion might send a requirement up to brigade and the brigade might pass that requirement up to the division. The division might pass the requirement laterally to a sister division and that division might pass it all the way down the chain to a subordinate company. In some cases a unit might pass a requirement to multiple assets and units. This level of complexity emphasizes why it is so vitally important for each unit to devote tireless effort to keeping requirement lists up to date.

Even with competent professionals exerting maximum effort, the intelligence process will never be perfect. This is another reason prioritization is critical. All the various intelligence requirements passing from one unit to another can quickly become overwhelming. It is the responsibility of intelligence professionals to filter and simplify their lists as much as possible in order to ensure that valuable intelligence does not get lost in a mass of noise. Another way to help reduce the complexity of communications traffic is to establish the second key element in for intelligence operation: the common operating picture.

Common Operating Picture

The common operating picture (COP) is essentially a one-stop shop for the most current and updated information. The idea behind the COP is that if every unit and collector compiles its updates in one place, then other units seeking information can potentially answer their questions without having to directly bother the collecting unit. However, it is still important that every posting include contact information for the collecting unit, in case consumers studying the COP have further questions.

If possible, each unit at each level of command should attempt to maintain its own common operating picture and to synchronize that picture laterally with peer units and vertically with subordinates and superiors. However, spending excessive time keeping the COPs synchronized can negate the advantage provided by the "one-stop shop" in the first place. Intelligence professionals must use their judgment to determine what information is relevant at each level and what level of synchronization is practical. Technology and computers can be useful in maintaining a consistent and accurate COP across multiple units and levels of command. However, it is still important to maintain and exercise redundant systems to avoid becoming overreliant on technology.

The effectiveness or ineffectiveness of the COP derives largely from format and presentation. Even the most complete and accurate COP is useless if it does not make it easy to quickly digest large amounts of information. Generally, a COP revolves around a digital or physical map with various labels and markings. There are many ways to organize information on the map to make it easier to absorb, including color coding, using commonly understood symbols, and attaching transparent folding overlays with labeled tabs.

Intelligence Products and Reports

The COP is only one example of an intelligence "product." A product is a polished compilation of critical information presented in an easily digestible, standardized format. As trivial as it might seem, one of the most decisive factors contributing to effective intelligence relates to the specific methods of formatting products. Formatting should make intelligence easily digestible and cause key information to naturally float to the surface. Good formatting also helps emphasize important patterns or linkages that might have otherwise escaped analysts' attention.

There are many creative ways of making intelligence products more useful and understandable. In general, the most useful methods allow analysts to visualize several patterns simultaneously. There are many historical examples for how such visualization methods helped improve situational awareness and command and control. In the Battle of Britain, the Royal Air Force used a special color-coded clock that allowed planners to instantly see how current each enemy aircraft sighting was simply by looking at the color of symbols on the map. Small formatting details like this can have a disproportionately powerful impact on success or failure.

There are many varieties of intelligence products, including link diagrams, pattern analysis wheels and terrain overlays, and a myriad of tips and tricks to make each product more useful and effective. Detailed examination of how and when to use each type of product is beyond the scope of this study. For the purpose of performance enhancement and assessment, the critical question is "What is each product used for?" The primary indicator of whether an intelligence product is effective is how many people actually use it to make decisions. If no one ever looks at an intelligence product, and the information contained in the product does not help drive decision making, the product is not serving any purpose and should either be modified or eliminated.

Other details such as the timing and formatting of periodic intelligence reports can prove equally important. There is no golden rule for how often units should submit reports. Most western armies that are obsessive about accountability submit reports too frequently. It is critical to judge every report's usefulness by determining how many people actually use it to make decisions. The appropriate timing and nature of reports depends on many factors and must constantly adjust to achieve the right balance of detail and streamlining.

There are a number of classic pitfalls that can make products and reports less effective. The first pitfall generally emerges when a unit insists on frequent reports with rigid report formatting. In such cases, each subordinate unit must fill out a daily report with several preformatted sections or categories. Over time, the task becomes mundane and is usually delegated down to a lower ranking officer with limited knowledge of the real situation. This officer will invariably have NSTR, or "nothing significant to report," on several sections of the daily report. However, if a unit turns in incomplete reports consistently, superiors will likely view this as laziness and order the unit to fill out each report completely, writing something in each preformatted section.

This encourages the reporting officer to fill the blank spaces with trivial or even fabricated information to avoid reprimand, which causes major problems for higher-level intelligence analysts sifting through numerous lower-level reports trying to put together an accurate intelligence picture. The critical and accurate information gets lost among the countless generalizations and fabrications encouraged by poor reporting formats and procedures.

There is no foolproof solution to this sort of problem. The problem is a typical example of the progressive deterioration of functionality due to an abundance of process-driven thinking and an absence of real thinking. Changes in reporting procedures and encouraging a culture of accurate reporting can help reverse the trend. Generally, the better model is to demand formal reports less frequently but devote greater attention to scrutinizing and analyzing each report. Less frequent formal reports will also encourage more informal reports, which are often more timely and relevant.

THE BATTLE FOR INTELLIGENCE

Intelligence is not just a set of procedures that supports the planning and operations process. Intelligence is a constant and ongoing battle between two thinking opponents. Each opponent seeks to steal the enemy's information while safeguarding friendly secrets. It is much more useful to look at intelligence in this light, as a separate battle unfolding simultaneously alongside the physical battle. Each battle is separate but the two battles interact and influence each other constantly. The mechanics of the intelligence system just described are only half of the intelligence equation. The other half is learning to plan, fight, and win the battle for intelligence against a hostile adversary.

Denial, Deception and Offensive Counterintelligence

The intelligence contest becomes exceedingly complex after factoring in the living, thinking opponent. The same level of complexity and core principles applies to any type of intelligence operation, whether hunting terrorists in times of peace or planning aerial reconnaissance in a time of war. As noted, intelligence is inherently complex because it is almost never perfect, and even if it is accurate, the situation is constantly changing. More complexity enters the equation when considering the living, thinking opponent who is attempting to deny, deceive and counter every intelligence effort.

Denial is the most straightforward form of countermeasure against intelligence. Planners too often depend on being able to collect the intelligence needed to plan an operation. This false sense of security grows more powerful when leaders are used to operating in permissive environments in which aerial assets are never shot down and technical collection means are never jammed or spoofed. Things become much more difficult when a leader sends a reconnaissance flight to photograph enemy positions and the aircraft is shot down. Does planning stop? Does the enemy now know friendly intentions? Is there time to send another flight? Are there other ways to collect the intelligence?

Shooting down reconnaissance aircraft is just one way to deny an adversary access to intelligence. It is also possible to hide information behind physical or technical barriers, or to jam sensors attempting to collect information. Implementing and enforcing good operational security is an effective way to deny the enemy access to human intelligence (HUMINT). These are just a few examples of denial, passive measures intended to deny the adversary access to intelligence.

Intelligence units must carefully consider all known and potential denial efforts and capabilities on both sides and factor them into all aspects of defensive and offensive planning. This means that in addition to the blocks intelligence officers must complete on the requirements sheet, each requirement also becomes an actual operation with associated risks and chances for success or failure. Before tasking collection assets, intelligence professionals must consider how enemy denial capabilities might jeopardize mission success.

Deception can be even more dangerous than denial. If a force falls prey to denial, at least it knows what it does not know. If a force falls prey to an effective deception, it does not know what it does not know. This ignorance can lead planners down the wrong path or directly into an enemy trap. Deception involves feeding the enemy false information, or allowing the enemy to find the intelligence they are looking for but ensuring that intelligence is inaccurate or misleading. A deception itself is an operation that must be planned and executed down to the smallest detail. For one thing, if false information is too easy to obtain, the enemy will likely guess that it was deliberately planted as a deception. It is usually necessary to make the enemy work for the false information in order to make the ruse believable.

Deception operations also demand supporting denial efforts to ensure that the enemy does not uncover the deception. For example, Operation Fortitude was an Allied deception operation that led the Germans to believe that the invasion of Europe would come at Pas-de-Calais instead of Normandy. The operation involved creating fake armies and positioning countless mock-up and inflatable tanks along the English coast for German reconnaissance aircraft to photograph. However, had it not been for an intricate web of British denial and counterintelligence efforts, including the turning of numerous German spies, the Germans may have had little trouble exposing the deception. Denial is an essential part of ensuring that deception works.

The British in the Second World War offer an excellent case study in offensive counterintelligence. While denial and deception are more passive and defensive in nature, offensive counterintelligence seeks to aggressively attack, destroy or turn enemy intelligence assets. There are many ways to do this. One way is to use coercion or blackmail to turn enemy agents against their former masters. Running a double agent frequently involves feeding the agent some accurate intelligence to establish the agent's credibility so the enemy will bite on false intelligence later on. The same applies when feeding information to enemy sensors or signal collection platforms.

Intelligence analysts and planners on both sides must consider the insidious effects of offensive counterintelligence when collecting intelligence for any operation. Attempting to use intelligence to make decisions becomes infinitely more complex in light of the fact that any given piece of intelligence might prove inaccessible or might be a deception. To make matters worse, the enemy might be aggressively targeting friendly intelligence assets and capacity. The above examples are not all-inclusive and are intended only to paint a general picture of the infinite complexities involved in the battle for intelligence. Such revelations are particularly useful in an age when some theorists mistakenly believe that technology will make it possible to attain perfect intelligence.

Reconnaissance and the Fight for Intelligence on the Battlefield

According to a U.S. Army saying, "Reconnaissance can be cheap, quick or thorough…now pick two out of three!" Essentially, reconnaissance can have any two of the above qualities but never all three. It can be quick and cheap but it will not be thorough. It can be cheap and thorough but it will not be quick. It can be quick and thorough but it will not be cheap in terms of casualties. This useful saying helps capture the true nature of reconnaissance on the battlefield. Heavily camouflaged scouts moving stealthily through the brush is only one form of reconnaissance. The fast pace and uncertainty of war often call for much more aggressive and violent ways of fighting for information.

Just as any intelligence operation must contend with counterintelligence efforts, battlefield reconnaissance rarely has a free hand to observe and report on enemy formations. Both sides take measures to prevent opposing reconnaissance elements from collecting useful information. Unit of all sizes will generally push smaller elements out and away from the main formation to act as guard or screening elements. These guard and screening elements are often the same units that perform offensive reconnaissance as well. Thus, in most cases, the opening moves of any battle are clashes between reconnaissance elements.

If one unit is executing a deliberate attack on a fixed enemy position, that unit will most likely send out reconnaissance elements to scout ahead. However, if the enemy is prepared, the enemy will have positioned defensive observation posts surrounding their defensive positions. The reconnaissance elements will run into the observation posts and a fight will ensue. It is therefore possible for neither force to see the other until one side wins the battle between reconnaissance forces.

It is difficult but possible to use stealth and misdirection to penetrate the enemy's screen or to deflect enemy reconnaissance elements without fighting. This is the ideal outcome for reconnaissance because the enemy is unaware that reconnaissance elements have compromised their positions. If an enemy force knows it has been spotted, it will react accordingly, taking evasive and defensive action to preempt an opposing countermove. If an enemy force does not know it has been spotted, it will blindly continue its current activities, leaving itself open to a surprise or trap. Again, while this might be the gold standard for reconnaissance, it is very difficult and risky to achieve.

In most cases, reconnaissance elements will clash and will begin reporting information back to their headquarters as quickly as possible. The reconnaissance elements will have to quickly destroy the opposing reconnaissance elements and may attempt to penetrate deeper into enemy lines in order to spot the main enemy force. With this scenario in mind, most modern reconnaissance units focus heavily on mobility and standoff firepower. Reconnaissance elements need to be able to put up a ferocious fight for a very short period of time to allow them to collect the information they need. Then they need to be able to move much faster than other units in order to be able to break contact and escape before the enemy can bring superior combat power to bear.

These points intend to illustrate that reconnaissance is not only an operation in itself but is also its own battle, sometimes separated from the main battle in time or space. Reconnaissance must be planned as a battle, complete with all the elements necessary for battle planning. This applies not only to ground reconnaissance units but also to air reconnaissance units. The enemy will make an effort to prevent air reconnaissance from breaking through, using ground-based air defense and combat air patrols.

Relating to these points, non-reconnaissance units can prove equally useful in gathering intelligence and updating the battlefield picture. Well-trained militaries enforce the practice of ensuring every soldier and every unit helps collect intelligence. Doing this effectively relates back to the requirements list discussed earlier in this chapter. Intelligence personnel can assign intelligence requirements to regular units as well as to dedicated intelligence assets. These priority intelligence requirements (PIR) are usually disseminated down to subordinate formations as part of the orders process. It is critical for every soldier in a formation to know the PIR by heart and to be ready to report findings up the chain of command.

The Art of Intelligence and Common Pitfalls

Most of the discussion to this point has offered general insights on the mechanical aspects of intelligence, which should be sufficient to help practitioners create a mechanically functional intelligence system. However, of all the defense and security disciplines, intelligence is one of the most challenging and complex. Even if practitioners follow all of the above points to the letter, the possibility of catastrophic failure is still very real. Intelligence is an inexact science and depends as much on intuition, risk taking and luck as it does on functioning systems.

While it is impossible to offer prescriptive advice for mastering the art of intelligence, as with all other arts, the best way to improve is constant practice. If practical application is not an option, running through countless historical case studies provides a form of passive practice that can help build intelligence game sense and intuitive pattern recognition ability.

Historical wargaming is particularly useful for learning the intelligence trade. It is even more effective when a trainee deliberately remains ignorant of real historical outcomes and realities. If a trainee does not know how a historical campaign actually played out, an instructor can provide the trainee with only partial information, limited to the perspective of what was available at the time and without the benefit of hindsight. The trainee can then conduct analysis and make predictions. Once the exercise is complete, the abundance of data available in hindsight allows the trainee to see if the predictions were correct. Essentially, one can use historical data as an answer key.

Certain types of people are ideally suited to the intelligence field, while others are not. Smart and flexible recruitment procedures and the ability to recognize talent are particularly important. The best intelligence collector or analyst might not be the person with the highest rank or most experience. It is equally important to incentivize and promote intelligence personnel whose predictions prove consistently accurate. Sometimes organizations harbor resentment towards such individuals and attribute their accuracy to luck. Lucky or not, intelligence personnel who get it right should move to positions of greater responsibility.

There are common pitfalls that can drastically reduce the effectiveness of intelligence. If an organization or unit does nothing else but strive to avoid these pitfalls, it will dramatically increase its chances of success. The first pitfall is mirror imaging. There is an overwhelming temptation to attempt to explain the enemy's actions by looking through the lens of one's own bias and perspective. Except in the most straightforward tactical scenarios, asking the question "What would I do if I were the enemy?" is often tragically misguided. It is not enough to put oneself in the enemy's shoes. One must strive to see the world through the enemy's eyes.

The second pitfall is overconfidence. Possibly the most common mistake in warfare is to assume that the next war will be a quick war or an easy war. Given the number of times such predictions have proved tragically wrong, it is remarkable that planners repeatedly make the same mistake. If someone makes a claim that a war will be quick, easy, or over in a specified amount of time, the statement should immediately set off warning alarms. The next questions should be: What is the worst case scenario? What if the war is not over in six months?

The final pitfall builds from the previous one of overconfidence. In some cases, intelligence analysts are overly optimistic because they are telling leaders and policymakers what they want to hear. This problem is particularly prevalent for organizations and societies in which individuals can be punished for reporting bad news. Both intelligence personnel and the intelligence consumers they serve must strive to avoid encouraging inaccurate reporting in this way. Intelligence personnel should never be punished for telling a leader what he or she does not want to hear. Consumers must be open minded and use intelligence to drive planning and policy, rather than use a predetermined policy as a guideline for which intelligence to focus on. Intelligence personnel must also always be courageous and dare to "speak truth to power." Failing to do so can have catastrophic affects at the national level.

Planning

The discussion of planning naturally follows the discussion of intelligence, since intelligence drives planning. When intelligence is done well, much of the work of planning is already done. However, there are still several critical factors, unique to the planning process, that can cause a plan to prove either effective or ineffective.

Planning Timeline and Backward Planning

Besides developing and updating the intelligence requirements list as discussed in the previous chapter, the first thing any planner must do is create a timeline. This timeline must incorporate every activity connected with the planning process. Time is so important because of the high degree of uncertainty in warfare. Many modern militaries assume timelines will remain constant during planning exercises. If planners are given 48 hours to develop a plan for an operation, they assume they will get the full 48 hours. Few militaries conduct exercises in which planners assume they have 48 hours to plan, only to discover unexpectedly that they must launch the operation after only 4 hours of planning.

In real military operations of all types, such unexpected surprises are not uncommon. Sometimes changing conditions force units to launch operations ahead of schedule. In other cases, unexpected events and distractions may rob units and planners of large portions of their programmed planning and preparation time. In high intensity conflict, the enemy might even bomb the headquarters where the plan is being developed. Essentially, when sitting down to start planning an operation in a real war, a planner never knows how much time he/she will have before execution time.

Keeping this in mind forces planners to front-load the most important planning and preparation activities. The first question must be: "If we have to move out and execute this plan in the next 15 minutes, what are the most critical planning and preparation tasks to complete in the 15 minutes we have?" In reality, many planning doctrines take almost the opposite approach. Much of the important work is saved for the end, which means that if the timeline unexpectedly accelerates, planners only will have completed mundane, preparatory work that will have little impact on success or failure.

A good analogy relates to planning a counterterrorism hostage rescue operation. If at any point the terrorists start killing hostages, the rescue team must be prepared to execute the assault immediately. The team cannot afford to block off 3 hours to develop a plan, but rather must develop a hasty plan as quickly as possible. If the terrorists start killing hostages immediately, at least the team will have something to execute. Once this hasty plan is complete, it buys the team time to convert the hasty plan into a more deliberate plan, focusing on the most critical planning and preparation tasks first.

The same principle applies to conventional warfare and all to other types of military or security operations. When establishing a defensive position, a unit should first establish a hasty defense and a hasty defensive plan. After achieving a reasonable degree of security, more deliberate planning can follow. When planning an offensive operation, the hasty plan might be a defensive plan to react to an enemy spoiling attack. In other cases, when an offensive move is critical, the hasty plan might itself be a spoiling attack or an attack with limited objectives. The main purpose of hasty planning is to ensure that a unit is never caught completely flatfooted.

After planners begin to front-load the most important planning activities, they must use the existing timeline and planning horizons to attempt to fit all of the necessary activities into the available time window. This timeline might change at any moment, but if it does not change, planners should be able to complete a detailed and comprehensive plan in the allotted time. Backward planning identifies the time that a unit must execute an operation and works backward to the present moment, ensuring there is enough time for all necessary planning and preparation activities.

Planners must carefully record every activity on the planning timeline. Key intelligence requirements and the expected time it will take to collect critical pieces of information can also appear on the timeline. If vehicle maintenance is required that will take 3 hours, those 3 hours must appear on the timeline as well. Sleep periods, guard rotations and resupply, every activity must appear on the timeline. Ensuring this level of detail will prevent planners from misallocating available time, running out of time for critical activities, or failing to execute the operation according to schedule.

If unexpected distractions or delays occur, those too must fit on the timeline, and will help planners decide which activities to shorten or which activities to eliminate in order to stay on schedule. The critical point is not to eliminate the most important activities. Since all activities should already be prioritized and progressing in priority order, this task should be easier to accomplish. However, some units fail to manage time properly and end up neglecting important priorities.

A common example of such an error is when units experience delays in the planning process and catch up with the timeline by eliminating rehearsals and inspections. Most military professionals agree that rehearsals and inspections are two of the most critical activities contributing to mission success. However, because these activities are often mistakenly placed at the end of the mission planning timeline, they often are cut off when delays emerge. If anything must be cut from the timeline, it should be the least important activity, not the most important.

Subordinate Unit Initiative in the Planning Process

One problematic aspect of many modern planning methods is that they start with the passive action of "receiving the mission." This reflects a top-down, hierarchical process associated with tightly synchronized, conventional operations. While some make the argument that "receiving the mission," can include coming up with an idea for a mission, word choices can have a powerful effect and the word "receive" is clearly passive in nature. Still, there are clearly times that warrant synchronized conventional operations, but the planning process should be flexible enough to adapt to all types of operations, including decentralized low-intensity conflict.

In low-intensity conflict and counterinsurgency operations, missions don't always come from the top down. Because units of company size and smaller are frequently spread across the area of operations, each unit must take the initiative to develop its own concepts for missions and operations. Sometimes missions will be dictated by higher headquarters, but some missions might begin with a platoon-level initiative that expands into a battalion-wide effort.

Small unit initiative can also prove useful in conventional operations, as long as forces are adequately trained in maneuver warfare, and commanders and subordinates share adequate trust. In such cases, it is not necessary for subordinate units to wait for orders before initiating their own plans. As long as it remains within the bounds of the commander's intent, a subordinate unit can capture fleeting opportunities on its own initiative. If a platoon must wait for orders from the company before taking the initiative, and the company must wait for orders from the battalion and so on, the timeline for making decisions becomes a slave to the decision-cycle speed of whatever unit is allowed to act on its own initiative. If the battalion commander is the only leader who can act on his/her own initiative, the platoon decision cycle can technically be no faster than the battalion decision cycle.

Additionally, if subordinates must check with higher commanders before acting, the number of decision interactions multiplies exponentially at each level of command. A battalion commander's decision cycle is inherently slower than a platoon leader's decision cycle. If the battalion commander must also verify the decisions of dozens of subordinate platoons, the cycle slows to a crawl. If opposing platoon leaders are able to act on their own initiative, they will be able to strike first while their opponents are waiting for higher approval.

Adding to the disadvantages of the top-down system, higher-level commanders attempting to micromanage subordinates are generally centrally located in a headquarters and therefore unable to see the real situation on the ground. Advanced sensors, communications equipment and drones cannot solve this problem; even if a commander could be "everywhere at once," the human brain would still prove unable to process all the information simultaneously.

Thus, in the sort of uncertain and time-constrained environments that usually characterize the modern battlefield, allowing lower-level units more leeway in the planning process drastically improves the practical chances of developing cohesive and effective plans. Attempting to synchronize every piece of the military machine is simply too complex a task to perform under pressure and will most likely prove ineffective against an agile opponent.

Nonetheless, it is important to realize that decentralized command structures and small unit initiative are necessary evils. Given unlimited time and resources, even militaries with the most decentralized command cultures still take the opportunity to carefully orchestrate and synchronize operations. The Germans did not plan and execute the assault on Fort Eben-Emael off the cuff. Instead, they rehearsed the plan over and over until it ran like clockwork. This does not mean the Germans did not also build flexibility into the plan and rehearse contingencies, only that they did not shy away from the opportunity to plan a carefully scripted assault when time allowed.

Contrary to the claims of staunch advocates for either maneuver warfare or synchronization warfare, there is indeed a time and place for both. With respect to the advocates of synchronization, given the fog and friction of war, the decentralized maneuver warfare approach generally proves more appropriate. However, it is only possible to execute maneuver warfare effectively with forces that have trained for decentralized operations, have a culture of small unit initiative, and have strong bonds of trust between superiors and subordinates. Attempting to command poorly trained or untrustworthy troops with the sort of loose grip typical of maneuver warfare would likely result in chaos. Thus, some military forces, particularly Third World forces, are better off using synchronization as opposed to decentralization.

Flattening the Orders Process

Given the opportunity to capitalize on the time-saving effects of a more decentralized command structure, there are other ways to engineer the orders process to greatly simplify the planning equation. Top-down military planning methods actually intended the hierarchical, downward flow of orders to allow subordinate units to plan with greater freedom and initiative. The idea was that a company receiving the battalion order would then have the time and freedom to develop its own company-level concept for the mission, without excessive interference or unwanted input from the battalion.

In reality, in the interests of speed and simplicity, it is generally better to centralize the initial planning process as much as possible. Making planning and orders production more collaborative also allows for greater cross talk and dialogue, resulting in better plans. Thus, instead of the battalion planning in isolation and pushing various orders and updates down to the company and so forth, it makes more sense for a group of leaders at various levels to plan the mission collaboratively. Within the bounds of practicality, the greater number of leaders who can simultaneously participate in developing the plan, the better.

If a battalion commander devises his plan collaboratively with the company commanders, the company commanders can provide invaluable, real-time feedback. Each company commander knows his/her area of operations better than the battalion commander and can use this knowledge to make valuable contributions to the plan. The company commanders also benefit from having the battalion commander in the same room. They can ask the battalion commander questions about the big picture and quickly hash out allocation of various assets and resources with both the battalion commander and the other company commanders. If in some situations it is impractical or dangerous to have so many commanders in one room, it is possible to employ the same collaborative planning methods remotely, though face-to-face communication makes the process much easier.

These same principles apply to every level of command. Consolidating planning efforts dramatically increases the time available for each individual unit to refine the details of its plan and to conduct the vital rehearsals and inspections that help ensure mission success. Collaborative planning allows leaders to align the bulk of planning time with the level of command that faces the highest degree of complexity, whether that is at lower or higher levels. By avoiding fixed time allocations, flattening the orders process and conducting more collaborative planning in a centralized manner, it is possible to greatly shorten planning timelines and increase planning efficiency. In other cases when time is critical, there may be no choice but to direct a single level of command to do most of the planning work and then direct subordinate units in a more controlled manner. This technique may be the only option for forces that are not as capable of conducting decentralized operations.

Collaborative Planning

Flattening and simplifying the orders process allows for a greater degree of collaborative planning, which is is nearly always preferable to commanders developing plans in isolation. The only cases where collaborative planning is less effective are for military forces with low levels of professionalism that depend on tight control and discipline to prevent dysfunction and information leaks.

In most other cases, however, collaboration in the planning process greatly increases speed and often improves the overall quality of the plan. Regardless of whether a unit is equipped with a staff, the concept behind collaborative planning is to get as many participants in the planning process as possible. Planning for a brigade-level operation should include not only the brigade staff but also key subordinate commanders and staff members.

Company-level units and below can use the same process. Instead of a platoon leader developing a plan in isolation, he/she will task squad leaders to draft their portions of the scheme of maneuver. The platoon sergeant and platoon medic might come up with the medical evacuation plan while the radio operator develops the communications plan.

The platoon leader assigns specific personnel to develop other pieces of the plan. For example, one soldier in the platoon might be the "route planner." This soldier will plan the route for every mission and maintain a "routes book" that includes information on which roads and bridges can support which size of vehicle, which routes are more vulnerable to enemy ambush, etc. If the same soldier plans the route every time, all the platoon leader needs to do is issue the objective location and the route planner can immediately begin planning primary and alternate routes with no additional guidance.

If the platoon sergeant needs to plan possible locations for helicopter MEDEVAC along the mission route, there is no need to distract the platoon leader. Instead, the platoon sergeant can go directly to the routes planner to determine where to mark helicopter landing zones along the route. The platoon leader can step back and let subordinates interact laterally. The leader can keep track of all of the various planning efforts and keep the process from spiraling into chaos. While checking on the progress of subordinates, the leader also must focus on developing the central concept for the operation and the plan for defeating the enemy on the objective. The participation of subordinate commanders helps streamline this effort.

The same planning method applies at the highest levels of command. A battalion or brigade commander's role should be to synchronize, manage and inspire the efforts of subordinates. A leader who is aggressively engaged in the planning process can manage a much larger collaborative team than doctrine would advocate. More minds working on the problem and sharing in the planning process increases speed and reduces the need to brief the plan to subordinates later on, as many of the subordinates will have helped build the plan in the first place.

Risk Assessment, Course of Action Development and Contingencies

Risk assessment is one of the most critical components of planning, but it is often overlooked or misunderstood. Many planners mistakenly associate risk assessment with risk aversion, due to the way risk assessment is frequently incorporated into the planning process. Risk assessment is often limited to using a preformatted worksheet to identify potential hazards and assign each one a numerical risk level, then identifying controls to mitigate each risk and determine the residual risk level. In simple terms, the process involves identifying the main hazards for the operation and finding controls to reduce the risk of each of those hazards, so the residual risk level (the level after controls are implemented) is lower than the initial risk level.

There is nothing wrong with this process, but the process itself can cause planners to think about risk assessment in the wrong way. To make matters worse, many units use the same risk management process and worksheet for combat operations and also for mundane activities such as physical training events and family morale gatherings. These non-combat risk assessments may include items like assessing the risk that someone will get hit by a car and then controlling that risk by ensuring that everyone wears reflective vests. There is nothing wrong with being concerned about safety, but because planners conduct so many risk assessments for non-combat activities, they can develop habits for thinking about risk that carry over into combat and may encourage risk aversion.

When conducted correctly in a combat operation, instead of consisting of a single worksheet, risk assessment permeates every aspect of a plan and in many ways drives the planning process. Rather than encouraging risk aversion, the risk assessment process is supposed to help planners assume greater risk and develop bolder plans that have a higher chance of decisive success. Most of history's greatest military leaders were bold risk takers. In the words of John Paul Jones, America's first naval hero, "Those who will not risk cannot win." However, the true essence of risk assessment, as it is explained in this book, is better captured in a quote by General George S. Patton Jr.: "Take calculated risks. That is quite different from being rash."

Simply being rash and taking foolish or unnecessary risks is never a wise approach. The risk assessment process allows planners to take calculated risks that offer the maximum chance of success. In this way, risk assessment is similar to the thought process of an experienced card player. It is impossible to "win big" without assuming risk by placing large bets. The larger the bet (or risk), the greater the potential payoff of a winning hand. The essence of winning at cards is knowing how and when to "bet big" in a calculated and responsible way. Likewise, in military operations, decisive victory is often not possible without assuming risks. Planners must often assume great risk in one area in order to focus decisive effort in another area. In making such decisions, the risk assessment process helps planners draw the line between being bold and being rash.

The risk assessment process is inseparable from course of action development. While collaborative planning is the most effective means for developing the plan, the planning team must still have a methodology or framework for developing the specific course of action that forms the core of any plan. In simple terms, the course of action is the way the operation will unfold and the approach the force will take, the creative solution for defeating the adversary.

There are many different doctrinal approaches for course of action development. One of the most common is for the planning staff to develop multiple courses of action (usually two or three), compare those courses of action, and then select the best one—or create a new course of action combining the best aspects of each course of action. While this is a valid approach, it is not always the most efficient and effective way to develop a course of action.

The multiple courses of action approach can prove very effective if there is plenty of time to develop the plan and the various courses of action are crafted in complete isolation. The planning staff must divide into isolated cells and have no contact until the various courses of action are complete. This allows for multiple "fresh looks" at the operational problem. Identifying the similarities and differences of each course of action can be a very productive and educational experience when the various cells come together to share their work. Most importantly, this approach is one of the best ways to stimulate creative thinking and novel perspectives.

Some units try to employ the multiple course of action approach without developing the plans in isolation; or worse, the same planning staff develops all three courses of action. This often leads to the development of one "real" course of action and two "fake" courses of action, developed only to fulfill the requirement of drafting multiple options, without any expectation that they will be used. If planning cells are not isolated, the various courses of action begin to look more and more similar as ideas bleed from one course of action plan into another. Additionally, if there is not enough time to fully develop each course of action, the final product might end up being rushed or incomplete.

The solution is not to abandon the concept of developing multiple courses of action and instead to focus on a single course of action. Rather, the solution is to realize that the process of developing, comparing and selecting multiple courses of action is actually implicit in any thoughtful planning process. When planners decide that the best approach is to attack from the west, this implies that either consciously or subconsciously they considered the alternative of attacking from the east, compared the two options, and decided that an attack from the west was superior. Therefore, capturing the benefits of the multiple course of action approach in a streamlined form simply involves recognizing and encouraging thoughtful comparison and analysis of multiple options throughout the planning process.

While there is no fixed formula for comparing and selecting different options, the process hinges on the concept of risk assessment introduced at the beginning of this section. As different options emerge during the course of action development process, each option will carry with it various risks. Frequently, the more risky options will also offer the most decisive results. Bold commanders often choose to assume a high-level risk, or to risk in one area in order to concentrate maximum effort in another area. Returning to the example of the Battle of France in 1940, the German decision to attack through the Ardennes Forest assumed a great deal of risk, as the German columns would be moving in densely packed formations through restricted terrain, highly vulnerable to air attack. Many decisive victories throughout history resulted from plans that assumed a high degree of risk.

The risk assessment process ensures that risks are calculated and not rash, while guiding the development of countermeasures and contingencies to minimize risk as much as possible. Instead of using a single fixed checklist or worksheet, it can be more effective to get into the habit of identifying and analyzing risks for every phase and component of the operation and actually "writing" the risks into the plan itself. For example, there will be one set of risks the unit must deal with in the assembly area, but those risks will change during the movement phase to the objective. Risks might differ between different sub-units or elements participating in the operation. There may also be unique risks associated with specific decisions or events on the battlefield, such as the decision to call for artillery support.

There are many ways to identify and analyze risks and represent them either graphically or in written form. Planners can choose which methods work best for them, but the key point is for the process to drive the allocation of assets and planning resources in a simple and flexible manner. As planners compare various options and their associated risks, a course of action will begin to take shape. As the course of action solidifies, planners must identify risks for each phase and aspect of the operation, rank them in priority order, then apply effort to mitigate those risks.

Applying effort to mitigate risk involves devoting more planning time, personnel, thought, resources, and assets to a particular problem or hazard. For example, if speed is essential for victory, a mechanized unit may decide to assume risk by moving in the open along a major road. Given this course of action, the most critical risks during movement might include air attack or an ambush by enemy anti-tank guided missiles (ATGMs). When these risks are identified, planners might assign additional reconnaissance assets to reconnoiter the road, request additional air support, or develop contingency plans for responding to enemy action, and then devote more planning time to rehearsing those contingencies in particular.

In summary, while some planning methods take a relatively narrow view of risk assessment, focusing mostly on the possibility of accidents or friendly fire, this book takes a wider view, using risk assessment to drive every aspect of the planning process. Risk assessment helps planners to choose a course of action that is bold but not rash. Risk assessment identifies the most critical dangers and hazards associated with each phase of the operation and allocates planning time and resources to develop and rehearse contingencies to address each risk in order of priority. Without going through a deliberate risk-assessment process, it can be difficult for planners to focus time, resources and rehearsals on the key areas that will help avoid catastrophe and ensure mission success.

Briefings and Written Orders

The key consideration for any briefing or written order is that it actually serves a purpose and transmits information to subordinates. Many military forces publish operations orders that are hundreds of pages long with numerous annexes and attachments. This should immediately raise flags. What is the purpose of an order that is hundreds of pages long when human beings can only hope to internalize a few pages of information at a time? Some might suggest that the idea is for commanders to be able to reference the order during combat operations. That too is illogical; if the plan is so complex that commanders must follow a written script, it is probably too complex and inflexible to stand against the chaos of the battlefield or an aggressive adversary.

The same principle applies to long briefings that run for several hours. It is impossible for subordinates to internalize all of that information. The plan, whether written or briefed, must be essentially simple and use as many visual and physical cues as possible. Rather than a long, text-heavy, written order it is better to use a series of maps, sketches and timelines showing movements and actions in clear detail. Rather than a long briefing in an auditorium, it is better to conduct the briefing and rehearsal walk-through simultaneously, asking each subordinate what their key tasks are as opposed to telling them.

The order must be short and simple enough to have time to discuss contingencies. The orders process must also incorporate realistic rehearsals as much as possible. Ideally, units should rehearse multiple times before a mission with intelligence officers playing the role of the enemy, introducing unexpected variables and forcing commanders to respond accordingly. Such rehearsals can take place in the field or on tabletop maps using movable pieces. The key point is that the process must be realistic and dynamic, not simply a robotic regurgitation of written orders.

Such concepts may appear obvious on the surface, but the unfortunate truth is that some military forces continue to fall victim to the planning pitfalls just discussed and fail to implement proven techniques for collaboration, rehearsals and wargaming. When evaluating a military force's planning capability, it is not enough to evaluate doctrine or even the curricula at training schools. The key is to observe how units actually operate in the field and verify that they employ best practices. It is also important to realize that performance across a force is generally inconsistent. In most military forces, some units and commanders will perform brilliantly while others may prove completely dysfunctional.

Offense

The study of offensive operations naturally emerges from an understanding of intelligence and planning. Intelligence drives planning, and planning is particularly important for offensive operations. Offensive operations seek a positive objective and strive to change the battlefield situation. Ultimately, each offensive effort at the strategic, operational and tactical levels must tie in with the overall strategic theory of victory. The smallest tactical action must remain nested within the highest strategic objectives. Offensive operations must form an essential piece of a narrative that ends in victory. This might seem obvious on the surface, but all too often offensive operations are conceptualized arbitrarily and provide questionable contributions to strategic goals.

Objectives in the Offense

While there are many different ways to define or characterize offensive operations, this book uses the positive aim or objective to distinguish offense from defense. The objective of the defense never changes: survival. Defense is a reactive posture: preparations designed to preserve the force in the face of surprise attack, retain combat power, and buy time for future offensive operations. Once leaders begin focusing on positive aims or take proactive actions as opposed to reactive, the force has transitioned to the offense.

Objectives of offensive operations derive directly from the theory of victory detailed in the strategy chapter. Once strategists come up with a theory of victory to accomplish political goals and achieve favorable terms for war termination, operational planners must begin identifying clear objectives that will lead to successful fulfillment of the theory of victory. There are typically multiple objectives, laid out in a sequence, leading to the desired strategic and political outcome.

Determining these objectives is the first step in offensive planning and will define all other aspects of the offensive plan. Different objectives call for different approaches and allocations of resources. While there are theoretically an infinite number of possible objectives in war, objectives generally tend to fall into one of the following broad categories: breaking the enemy's will, deterrence, political de-legitimization, direct attack on the population, annihilation of the enemy force, capturing key terrain, attriting the enemy force, operational shock, resource strangulation, and regime change.

Breaking the Enemy's Will

Eventually, this is how all wars are won. It is virtually impossible to physically annihilate an entire enemy force, state and culture. Numerous historical examples and scientific studies confirm that as long as the will remains unbroken, the human capacity to endure, resist and fight back is nearly limitless. Therefore, the objective must always be to break the enemy's will to fight, to cause them to lose heart and give up. This maxim applies to every level of warfare from individual combat to grand strategy.

At the strategic level, breaking the enemy's will has less to do with causing individual enemies to give up and more to do with demoralizing the society as a whole and discouraging the state's political leadership. The French defeat in Algeria offers a good example of this. Though the French won the vast majority of tactical victories, the insurgent strategy was to degrade the political will of the French people and leadership to continue the conflict.

The same phenomenon led to the U.S. withdrawal in Vietnam. The U.S. military did not withdraw from Vietnam because of defeat on the battlefield, but rather because the American public and political leadership lost the will to continue fighting. Protracted guerrilla war such as those in Algeria and Vietnam is not the only way to break an enemy's political will. There are many ways to achieve the ultimate objective of breaking the enemy's political will both directly and indirectly, by focusing on intermediate objectives. The first of these intermediate objectives is deterrence.

Deterrence

Sometimes it is possible to break the enemy's will without engaging in battle. Deterrence involves intimidating the enemy so they decline to fight in the first place and instead agree to friendly political terms to avoid conflict. In some cases, deterrence simply aims to prevent an enemy from launching a first strike. The most well-known example of deterrence is the nuclear deterrence during the Cold War. The idea behind maintaining a nuclear arsenal was not to actually use it but rather to deter an enemy attack with the threatening prospect of nuclear war.

Deterrence applies to all levels of conflict, not solely nuclear warfare. Placing heavily armed police officers in subway stations is a form of deterrence. The first objective is to present such an intimidating posture that criminals or terrorists choose not to instigate violence in the first place. Erecting strong, menacing defensive positions might discourage an enemy attack in a conventional war. Advertising the capabilities of new weapon systems or technologies might make political leaders think twice before initiating conflict. Deterrence has countless applications at all levels of war, but its ultimate objective is to break the enemy's will to fight before conflict begins.

Political De-legitimization

This objective specifically targets the will of the enemy's political leadership. The way to achieve victory through this objective is commonly misunderstood. It is possible to de-legitimize an enemy leader to the point where he/she is overthrown. This objective, regime change, is different from political de-legitimization and will be discussed separately. Regime change is more complex and potentially problematic, as there is no guarantee that the new regime will not be more belligerent than the first. Successful regime change requires a delicate process of affecting the transition from an undesirable regime to a more favorable one.

Political de-legitimization targets the political will of the enemy leaders in power. Essentially, if the course of a conflict is causing a leader to grow increasingly unpopular, that leader might choose to end the conflict in order to preserve his/her own legitimacy. If a leader fears being replaced or overthrown, he/she is likely to do whatever is necessary to stay in power. Taking steps to make a leader increasingly unpopular and to associate that leader with negative developments in the conflict can trigger a political decision to stop fighting.

Direct Attack on the Population

This objective has taken many forms and has often proved ineffective--apart from being inherently unethical--when compared to other modes of warfare. While the traditional model of warfare (discussed next) articulated by Clausewitz calls for breaking the enemy's political will through the annihilation of the enemy army, an attack on the population attempts to bypass the enemy's military altogether and target the population's will to fight directly. One of the most common forms of this approach is the terror bombing of population centers. Both the Axis and Allies employed terror bombing, with the attacks on London, Dresden, Tokyo, Hiroshima and Nagasaki providing some of the most infamous cases.

Prewar air power theorists like Giulio Douhet anticipated that just a few air raids on population centers would have such an overwhelming effect on the population that peace talks would inevitably follow. The aim was to "terrorize" the population so they would demand an immediate, peaceful resolution. Variations on this approach relate to political de-legitimization as well. In an alternative scenario, the war ends because the threat of bombing angers the population and threatens the legitimacy of the leaders who are apparently unable to stop the bombers. The leaders must then sue for peace to appease the populace.

While this approach seemed logical in theory, numerous case studies of conventional terror bombing reveal that directly targeting an enemy population does not break the people's will but instead can even strengthen popular resolve. In the Second World War, the citizens of London did not panic or give up in the face of repeated German air attacks; instead, they united as a people to survive and rebuild. Direct attacks on the enemy population often prove to be ineffective.

The notable exception to this rule is the nuclear attacks on Hiroshima and Nagasaki. Employment of nuclear weapons did in fact bring the Japanese to the negotiating table. It is impossible to know the precise factors leading to Japanese capitulation, or whether nuclear weapons would have similar effects under other conditions. However, it is important to realize that nuclear weapons may be an exception to the rule that direct attacks on the population are ineffective.

Terror bombing is not the only way to attack the population directly. Terrorists attempt to use the same logic as terror bombing: attacking and demoralizing the civilian population through fear, eroding confidence in government and attempting to affect political change. The difference is that terrorists do not have access to strategic bombing forces and must instead use unconventional tactics like hijacking planes and planting bombs on buses or in populated areas.

An important distinction to keep in mind is that while conventional militaries often make an effort to avoid or at least justify the targeting of civilians, terrorists often make excessive cruelty an end in itself. Capturing and murdering hostages, in many cases publicly and using creatively brutal means, is one of the most heinous trends in modern terrorism and places many terrorist groups in their own category of moral depravity. It is also relevant to note that occupying armies and oppressive regimes throughout history, including the Nazis and Japanese in the Second World War, have used equally brutal methods to suppress and control resistance and popular uprising.

Annihilation of the Enemy Force

This is generally considered the classic objective of western warfare. Most western military theorists such as Carl von Clausewitz and Alfred Thayer Mahan posit that it is the physical destruction of the enemy army or navy in the field that offers the quickest path to victory. Destroying the enemy force in the field generally involves finding a way to fix the main body of the enemy force in place and then destroy it in a single, decisive engagement. As mentioned, Clausewitz did not consider the destruction of the enemy army an end in itself but rather a means for breaking the enemy's political will. Clausewitz suggested that the catastrophic defeat of an army in the field invariably causes the local population and political leadership to lose hope and sue for peace.

The key challenge of winning a war of annihilation is getting the enemy to accept battle under unfavorable conditions and to concentrate their forces in a way that will allow for their destruction. Most trained armies try to disperse their forces, explicitly to prevent their annihilation in a single decisive engagement. When faced with an overwhelming threat, a trained adversary will simply refuse battle and wait to fight under conditions that are more favorable. Therefore some sort of fixing effort, bait or deception is often required to get the enemy to irrevocably commit to a decisive battle that will end in their own destruction.

Using mobility and supporting fires to fix the enemy in place is one way to force the enemy to accept battle. Napoleon was one of the first commanders to apply this approach to modern warfare. His brilliant design and employment of highly mobile, independent corps allowed him to outmaneuver and fix the enemy army. German blitzkrieg tactics also used mobility to envelop large enemy formations in "cauldrons" to prevent their escape and allow for their complete destruction.

Deception is another way to get the enemy to accept battle under unfavorable conditions. If the enemy leader is plagued by hubris or overconfidence and believes that he/she has the advantage, it is possible to capitalize on this and trick the enemy into accepting battle. This approach has been used countless times at all levels of warfare. A classic example from small unit tactics is the "baited ambush," in which a small force will feign retreat to lure the pursuing enemy forward into the kill zone of a larger ambush. In other cases, this concept of "bait" can connect the objective of annihilation to terrain objectives.

Capturing and Holding Key Terrain

This objective is sometimes labeled as misguided or ineffective. However, the usefulness of capturing key terrain becomes clear when viewed in the context of additional objectives. For example, many armies have threatened or attacked an enemy capital with the intention of luring the opposing army into a decisive battle. This was the German logic for capturing Moscow. With Moscow threatened, the Russians would have no choice but to commit the bulk of their army to a decisive battle that the Germans could win.

The same logic applied to the German bombing of London. The primary objective was less to terrorize the population than to draw the RAF into a decisive air battle of annihilation.

In other cases, capturing and holding terrain is not intended as a prelude to a battle of annihilation. Capturing terrain is still not an end in itself, but terrain seizure and retention can provide other benefits or support to operations as a whole. There are countless examples of this. Controlling key road junctions may speed the flow of supplies to the front line. Controlling high ground can offer better positions for artillery spotters. Captured enemy supply depots and industrial infrastructure can be repurposed to serve friendly objectives.

Key terrain takes different forms in land, naval and air warfare, but the general concepts for planning terrain objectives are similar. In land warfare, terrain objectives might include crossroads, rail lines, ports, high ground, river crossings, urban areas and logistical assets. It is a common mistake for ground commanders to view key terrain as an objective in itself and not to think through how seizing and retaining key terrain fits into a larger operational plan.

In air warfare, the concept of key terrain is somewhat less varied. First, airspace itself is key terrain, and the battle for air superiority is not dissimilar from battles to control key roads and bridges. Just as controlling roads facilitates the maneuver of land forces, controlling the air facilitates air interdiction, air support, air reconnaissance and air transport.

Another form of key terrain in air warfare is air bases. The location of air bases is critical to all aspects of air warfare. An example of this is the island-hopping campaigns in the Pacific theater of the Second World War. A critical reason for invading each island was to capture its air base or terrain suitable for constructing an air base, to extend the range of U.S. aircraft. This extended range allowed air support for subsequent invasions of other islands. Expanded air coverage also allowed for more comprehensive air cover for naval forces and sea lines of communication. Proximity of air bases is critical, as it affects the amount of time fighters and bombers can spend over the target or in support of friendly forces. The farther aircraft must fly to get to the battle, the less time they will have to fight before their fuel runs out.

Naval warfare follows a similar pattern. Controlling key terrain in naval warfare consists largely of controlling sea lines of communication and chokepoints such as straits and canals. This relates to the ideas British naval historian Sir Julian Corbett advanced in his book Some Principles of Maritime Strategy, first published in 1911. The force that controls the sea lines of communication gains an advantage in the ability to transport and resupply forces by sea. Ports, like airfields, are key terrain, important for sustaining and maintaining the naval force.

These are only a few examples of how the concept of key terrain applies to all levels and domains of warfare. Some counterinsurgency theorists even relate the concept of capturing key terrain to winning the support of the local population in a counterinsurgency struggle. The key task for leaders is to weave the various terrain objectives together into a larger plan to defeat the enemy's force through annihilation, attrition or shock.

Attriting the Enemy Force

Attrition is the opposite approach to annihilation. While annihilation aims to destroy the bulk of the enemy force in a single, decisive engagement, attrition aims to wear the enemy force down over an extended period through multiple, smaller engagements. Choosing attrition over annihilation is often a necessity rather than a choice. Weaker forces that are not strong enough to face the enemy in decisive battle often resort to guerrilla warfare, never committing to open battle and instead using hit-and-run tactics to wear down the enemy over time.

Focus on attrition is often necessary in naval and air warfare, where the balance of ships and aircraft has a significant effect on the outcome of battle. In air warfare, for example, kill ratios are a critical measure of progress towards victory. A favorable kill ratio leads to an ever-increasing numerical advantage, which in turn yields an even more favorable kill ratio.

Essentially, the more enemy aircraft one side shoots down, the less aircraft that side will have to confront the next day. Therefore, neglecting attrition as an objective in air warfare can lead down a dangerous slope that ends in disintegration of the air force. Attrition is also important in naval warfare for the same reasons. The more ships one side sinks, the greater the growth in numerical advantage. It is very difficult and slow to build new ships, so it is difficult to reverse a dwindling numerical advantage in naval warfare.

While particularly relevant to air and sea warfare, attrition applies to all types of warfare to some extent. Even for a force that focuses primarily on winning through annihilation or shock, some attrition is inevitable and attriting enemy forces is always a subcomponent of any combat operation. Some forces may also choose to rely on attrition as a primary objective. If a force has significant superiority in numbers or industrial capacity, the most certain path to victory may be allowing both sides to wear each other down over time, knowing that numerical or industrial advantages will make the result inevitable. This was central to Ulysses S. Grant's approach in the American Civil War and also contributed to the Soviet victory over the Germans in the Second World War.

Operational Shock

In addition to the objectives of annihilating or attriting the enemy, a third option is to defeat the enemy by inducing operational shock. The term "operational shock" is usually associated with Soviet Deep Operations doctrine, but the same essential concept relates to German blitzkrieg campaigns and other fast-paced combat operations. Winning by inducing operational shock means targeting the enemy's decision cycle rather than focusing on the actual destruction of enemy forces. For instance, the objective of blitzkrieg was to penetrate deep into enemy territory as quickly as possible, outpacing the enemy's ability to react and spreading a condition of panic and confusion throughout the enemy force. It was this panic and confusion itself, not necessarily the physical destruction of enemy forces, that would ultimately trigger enemy collapse.

The concept of operational shock and how to induce it is perhaps best explained by the theories of Air Force Colonel John Boyd, articulated in his presentation "Patterns of Conflict." Boyd's theory states that all combat engagements consist of competitive Observe-Orient-Decide-Act cycles or "OODA loops." In combat, each side must continually observe enemy actions, orient to the situation, make a decision, and act on that decision. Action causes changes to the situation; both sides must observe the changes, reorient, make the next decision and act on it. In this way, the OODA loop repeats over and over in a decision cycle. Operational shock occurs when one side is able to continually cycle through the OODA loop faster than the adversary. As the adversary falls further and further behind in the decision cycle, the ability to make decisions eventually breaks down entirely. This state of paralysis is called operational shock because it is the operational system itself that is paralyzed.

A force paralyzed by operational shock can no longer fight effectively and cohesively on the battlefield and will inevitably crumble. Victory through operational shock is difficult to accomplish, as it usually requires a highly trained and highly mobile force. However, when compared to victory through attrition or annihilation, the results are typically much quicker and less costly.

Strangulation

In some cases, it might be possible to cut off an enemy's supply of critical resources or starve the enemy into submission through a naval blockade. This was the objective of German U-boat operations in the Second World War as well as of U.S. submarine operations against Japan. Against an island nation like Britain or Japan, it is theoretically possible to turn the tide of conflict by cutting off the flow of supplies from the sea. However, while the U.S. nearly succeeded in completely cutting off the flow of Japanese supplies, winning a war solely through strangulation is an unlikely prospect. Strangulation is more effective when applied in conjunction with other approaches.

The same rule applies to strategic bombing campaigns targeting enemy industry. While the combined bomber offensive in the Second World War might not have been able to secure victory on its own, it undoubtedly made a significant contribution to the war effort. The Allied approach sought to identify industrial chokepoints, based on the logic that the complete elimination of a single resource could cause the German war machine to break down entirely, while simultaneous reduction of several resources could only hope to degrade German capabilities. Allied planners focused on various "single points of failure," including ball-bearing production and ultimately oil and fuel production. While this approach never achieved the complete systemic breakdown it sought, reductions in German fuel stores undoubtedly aided Allied efforts in the later stages of the war.

Regime Change

Regime change is an extremely complex topic, and explaining the fundamentals for effective execution of a regime change operation is beyond the scope of this book. More detailed coverage of special operations, intelligence and unconventional warfare techniques must be reserved for later publications. However, there are a few key insights relating to regime change that are worth discussing in a more general sense.

Regime change calls for overthrowing and replacing the leader or ruling regime of a hostile country. While attempts at regime change are not uncommon in the modern international system, achieving acceptable strategic outcomes through regime change can be very difficult. The most serious challenge is making sure that the new regime ends up being more favorable to overall political objectives than the old regime. There are many examples in history where ousting one leader brings an even less desirable figure into power.

Ensuring a smooth transition to a more desirable regime requires a great deal of preparatory work: identifying and vetting potential replacements for the existing regime, discretely providing political advice or financial support, crafting information campaigns, and identifying and degrading opposition capabilities. All of these efforts are particularly difficult as they must be conducted covertly in a denied area. Furthermore, most regimes worth overthrowing impose very tight control on their populations and have highly capable, or at the very least ruthless, internal security forces.

A final additional complication is that if any evidence of foreign influence or covert action is detected, it can backfire catastrophically, proving counterproductive to political and diplomatic interests. Therefore, while regime change is indeed possible, it is a more challenging undertaking than many leaders are willing to admit. A large volume of analysis, wargaming and critical thinking should precede any efforts to pursue regime change in a hostile country.

Multiple Objectives

Planners will rarely focus solely on a single objective, and it is generally poor practice to do so. Instead, planners will lay out a series of objectives that may be accomplished either in sequence, simultaneously, or a combination of both. In some cases, accomplishing one objective will make the next objective easier. In 1940, the Germans realized that defeating the Royal Air Force was an essential prerequisite to facilitate any cross-channel invasion of Britain.

There is an advantage to pursuing multiple objectives simultaneously. While on the surface it might seem logical to focus all available effort toward a single objective, doing so provides the enemy with a simple, one-dimensional problem and reduces the friendly ability to adapt to changing circumstances. Simultaneously pursuing multiple objectives allows leaders to shift effort from one objective to another should they meet stiff resistance or achieve inadequate results.

Identifying and arraying objectives over time is a critical component for mission success at all levels of warfare. It is possible to incorporate all the various types of objectives explained above into a single operational concept. A conflict might begin with efforts to deter the enemy. If deterrence fails, the next effort might be political de-legitimization through a decisive battle of annihilation. If that fails to offer the desired result, planners might resort to an attrition campaign while buying time to explore other options, and then eventually defeat the enemy through operational shock while simultaneously degrading enemy resources through strategic bombing.

These same core categories of objectives have numerous applications in a wide variety of scenarios. There are other possible objectives in combat operations, particularly when expanding the scope of operations beyond conventional warfare into areas such as unconventional warfare, special operations, counterterrorism and law enforcement. Nonetheless, the same principles for identifying and sequencing objectives apply to any form of combat operation. Once objectives are identified, the next step is to choose the operational methods to accomplish each objective.

OPERATIONAL METHODS

It is first critical to note that "operational methods" do not solely relate to the operational level of war but rather could apply to any level of war. An operational method is a specific approach to

Offense **143**

accomplishing an objective. Just as there are an infinite number of possible objectives in warfare, there are also an infinite number of operational methods that can be used to accomplish those objectives. Still, there are some common operational methods that are worth discussing, as they have featured in a large number of contemporary wars.

It is also important to note that while operational methods suggest a more nuanced, calculated approach to accomplishing objectives, it is also possible to pursue any of the objectives already discussed in a more blunt fashion. For example, it is possible to wage a war of attrition, and even win it, simply by launching as many bodies into the fight as possible. Such approaches do not really include a "method" at all so they are not discussed in the following section. It is also important to note that methods are not mutually exclusive and it is possible to use combinations of several methods.

Combined Arms

Combined arms has largely become the accepted operational method in modern warfare and is either included in or related to most of the other methods discussed here. Combined arms calls for integrating the effects of two or more "arms" on the battlefield. For example, the combined employment of infantry, tanks and artillery qualify as combined arms. However, the defining quality of combined arms is that the effect of multiple arms used in combination must be greater than the effect if each arm was used separately. Essentially, the combination of various weapons and capabilities proves mutually complementary and yield a greater overall impact.

In ideal circumstances, combined arms are not only complementary but also place the enemy in a dilemma where defending against one arm will expose them to another. A typical example from the Cold War was the tactic of integrating anti-armor minefields with anti-tank guided missiles, providing cover or "overwatch." As tanks approached the minefield, they needed to slow down to avoid the mines. However, to avoid the incoming ATGMs, the tanks needed to speed up and take evasive action.[29] Countering one arm increases exposure to the other.

While generating such a dilemma is not always possible, it is useful to ensure that the various arms support each other in the most effective way and attempt to offset each other's weaknesses. For example, it is better to attack air defense installations with infantry when possible. Each formation or weapon system on the battlefield is particularly vulnerable to certain other formations or weapon systems under given conditions. Tanks are vulnerable to infantry in an urban environment, while infantry are vulnerable to tanks in the open. One goal of combined arms is to attempt to employ each arm in a way that capitalizes on that arm's strength while exploiting the enemy's weakness.

Maneuver Warfare vs. Synchronization Warfare

Maneuver warfare and synchronization warfare are common operational methods that relate primarily to different approaches to the orders process and command and control. Maneuver warfare is generally associated with the German army, particularly the blitzkrieg campaigns of the Second World War, and has since been expounded upon and popularized by the late U.S. Air Force Colonel John Boyd. Synchronization warfare traces its roots to three inter-war Soviet military theorists, later contributed to Soviet victory in the Second World War, evolved into the Cold War Soviet Deep Operations doctrine, and eventually influenced the creation of the U.S. Army's Air-Land Battle doctrine.

While maneuver warfare and deep operations are frequently cited by military professionals, misconceptions exist about each approach. One of the most common misconceptions about maneuver warfare is that its opposite is attrition warfare. Labeling maneuver warfare and attrition warfare as opposites does not make logical sense. It is possible to use maneuver warfare to accomplish attrition-based objectives; therefore, the two cannot be antithetical. As stated, the essence of maneuver warfare primarily relates to command and control. Therefore, the opposite of maneuver warfare must be the opposite method of command and control: synchronization warfare.

The basis of maneuver warfare is decentralization and the empowerment of subordinate leaders to act on their individual initiative. The basis of synchronization warfare is centralized control and disciplined execution. However, these opposite command and control methods ultimately seek victory in the same way. Most victories on the battlefield stem principally from two factors: speed and power. In simple terms, there are primarily two ways to win a fight: hit first, or hit harder and more effectively. Maneuver warfare and synchronization warfare both pursue these same goals in different ways.

Speed in maneuver warfare comes from decentralized execution and subordinate initiative. The maneuver warfare force beats the enemy to the punch by allowing subordinates to act immediately and decisively without wasting time seeking higher approval for each action. The maneuver warfare force achieves power superiority (manpower, firepower or combat power) only locally. By definition, a decentralized command structure moving in multiple columns cannot mass to achieve overall superiority. However, using the more decentralized approach of "recon pull," reconnaissance units can "pull" a maneuver force behind them along the path of least resistance, identify weak points in the enemy lines, then use superior agility to quickly mass power at those points, achieving local superiority and facilitating a breakthrough.

Speed in synchronization warfare comes from highly synchronized and disciplined execution. While initiative and creativity are not paramount, a force can still potentially outpace an adversary if the military machine runs flawlessly. Synchronization warfare achieves power superiority by synchronized massing of combined arms capabilities on the largest possible scale. A synchronization force will often have large, centralized staff employing a complex system of control measures, timelines, execution checklists and matrices.

While both methods are ultimately about achieving superiority in speed and power, the historical record shows that the maneuver warfare approach is clearly superior for one key reason: the inherent uncertainty of warfare. If nothing ever went wrong on the battlefield and events always proceeded as planned, the synchronization warfare force would win every time. However, this is never the case and accordingly, when things go wrong, the maneuver warfare force gains a tremendous advantage due to its superior adaptability. In reality, not only is a synchronization warfare force less flexible and adaptable, but frequently the better a force gets at synchronization, the less adaptable it becomes.

If maneuver warfare is clearly superior, why would a force ever employ synchronization warfare? There is indeed a reason. The central challenge of maneuver warfare is getting all of its decentralized pieces to function in harmony. High levels of training and mutual trust between superiors and subordinates are essential for achieving this harmony. Many forces are simply not capable of executing maneuver warfare because they are not trained for maneuver warfare. Allowing highly trained, competent subordinates to act on their own initiative will likely bring good results. Empowering poorly trained and incompetent subordinates will likely lead to chaos. Thus, less experienced units that do not place great emphasis on training for maneuver warfare are sometimes better off relying on synchronization.

Targeting

While maneuver warfare and synchronization warfare are operational methods that relate primarily to different approaches to command and control, effective targeting depends on the integration of timely intelligence and the rapid delivery of munitions or strike forces on a target. There are several different terms for targeting; some of them relate to different targeting methods or apply to different types of conflict. However, this section uses the general term "targeting" to discuss underlying principles common to most targeting methods.

Targeting relates less to fluid maneuver on the battlefield and more to the effective application of strategic bombing, airstrikes, precision guided munitions and surgical strike units. Some modern militaries have the capability to strike targets anywhere in the world using a myriad of munitions fired from a diverse collection of platforms including aircraft, ships and submarines. However, by necessity, there is a limit to the number of targets a force can service in a given time period. Effective targeting calls for thoughtful prioritization, finding and fixing targets, then servicing them in priority order.

An example of a good, or at the very least thoughtful, targeting effort goes back to the Allied combined bomber offensive in the Second World War. Intelligence analysts and planners developed a meticulous list of targets and established methodologies for prioritizing those targets in such a way as to maximize the available strike resources and cause the greatest damage to the enemy system. In comparison, German bombing efforts during the Battle of Britain were completely disjointed and often appeared random. There was generally no logic behind the selection or sequencing of ground targets, and the unimpressive results likely contributed to subsequent German defeat.

Effective target selection and prioritization hinges on timely and accurate intelligence. A contemporary example of this, relating to an entirely different type of targeting, is the special operations counterterrorism campaigns in Iraq, Afghanistan and around the globe. A key factor that made these operations successful was not only the skill and courage of the special operations personnel but also the streamlined cycle of intelligence exploitation, analysis and dissemination that accelerated the tempo of operations and allowed for rapid deconstruction of terrorist networks.

The seamless integration of intelligence and operations is critical to all forms of targeting, not solely special operations targeting. The force that collects and analyzes information faster and can strike first quickly gains the upper hand. If the targeting campaign is well planned and target selection and sequencing is thoughtful, the barrage of strikes can rapidly degrade enemy capabilities and force the enemy into a reactive mode, from which they will be unlikely to regain the initiative.

INITIATIVE IN THE OFFENSE

Offensive operations usually generate more uncertainty than defensive operations, are more difficult to control, and thus tend to incur greater risk. Unlike defense, where if time allows it is ideal to meticulously think through every possible contingency and make defensive preparations as complete as possible, in the offense speed and initiative must often substitute for control and security. This point is worth mentioning because many offensive planners attempt to impose unrealistic degrees of certainty on offensive plans. Countless "what if" questions emerge about potential enemy countermoves, and the planning staff proceeds to attempt to create a plan that accounts for all of them. Efforts to create such a watertight plan, besides being impossible, lead to plans that are excessively cautious and scripted.

Offensive planners need to take refuge in the conviction that aggressiveness and initiative alone are enough to prevent the enemy from striking back effectively. The key for the offense is always to maintain the initiative and to dictate the terms of the battle. It can be very difficult to predict enemy actions but it is much easier to predict enemy reactions. By striking first and continuing to strike, forcing the enemy to constantly react to friendly moves, it is possible to achieve nearly complete control of the enemy's actions. Such an enemy will become overwhelmed and immediately turn focus inward to keep its force and command structure from breaking down. It will not have time to plan effective countermoves.

Simultaneity

A critical factor in seizing and maintaining the initiative is simultaneity. The reason for this is that most military forces attempt to maintain certain units in reserve to prevent their entire force from becoming overwhelmed at one time. Competent planners will array their forces so that even if part of the force is getting overwhelmed, other units or reserve forces remain farther back from the action and retain the initiative to execute an effective countermove.

The concept of simultaneity in the offense strives to strike all enemy elements simultaneously, keeping the entire enemy force off balance and preventing reserves from executing effective countermoves. In conventional warfare, simultaneity can be achieved by rapid mobile or air-mobile penetration into the enemy rear areas. Rather than taking the more cautious approach of a measured advance, forces must race as far into the enemy rear as possible, striking and paralyzing the full depth of the enemy force. Forces that cannot be assaulted simultaneously should be at a minimum fixed, or degraded through air and artillery attack.

One of the key principles for success in military operations is concentration of forces to achieve local firepower superiority. The benefits of concentration must balance with the importance of simultaneity. Attacking at multiple points implies some dispersion of effort; however, the paralyzing effects of such a broad attack generally outweigh the disadvantages of dispersion. If a unit concentrates all of its forces along a single axis, regardless of how devastating the attack proves to be, the enemy is presented with a very simple operational equation. The enemy knows where all of the opposing forces are and will probably attempt to counterattack or retreat, refusing to let all of their forces be destroyed in a single clash.

There are times when it is appropriate to focus all effort at a single point, particularly when the momentum and speed of the attack will outpace enemy efforts to respond. Nonetheless, in most cases, attacking simultaneously along multiple axes or stacking multiple echelons in depth will achieve better results. Multiple thrusts present the enemy with a more complex problem, slowing enemy decision cycles and taxing enemy intelligence, command and control. In addition, multiple thrusts offer friendly forces the opportunity to shift the main effort from one thrust to another based on enemy reactions or situational changes.

Local Superiority and Defeat in Detail

Balancing the advantages of simultaneity is the concept of local superiority. The effort to achieve local superiority forms the basis for many modern tactical and operational techniques. To offer an analogy, if two fighters in a ring square off against three fighters of equal skill, the result is predictable. A single fight of three against two will likely go in favor of the group of three.

However, what if the fight is not taking place in a ring but instead the fighters are spread out inside a building? The group of two fighters choose to stay together and stay mobile while the group of three fighters decide to spread out and wait in different rooms. In this case, the group of two fighters can use their concentrated force and superior mobility to defeat each of the three opponents one at a time. Instead of fighting outnumbered in a two vs. three fight, the two fighters fight a two vs. one fight three separate times, ganging up on each isolated opponent individually.

In this example, the group of two fighters might have been outnumbered overall but they still managed to outnumber their opponents in each successive fight, achieving a local superiority in each case. A classic historical example of this phenomenon was the Battle of Thermopylae, in which a small number of Spartans were able to inflict serious damage on a much larger Persian force because the terrain made it impossible for the Persians to bring their entire force to bear. This technique can apply in all types of conflict. By concentrating forces against isolated elements of the enemy force one at a time, it is possible for a smaller force to defeat a larger force. This is also called "defeat in detail."

Mobility in Offensive Operations

One of the most challenging offensive problems, particularly in land warfare, is the difficulty of moving large forces long distances through enemy territory. While this delves into lower-level operational and even tactical details, it is central to the overall concept of the offense and important enough to warrant careful examination. Offensive planners sometimes focus only on the objective itself and fail to realize that any offensive operation is a fluid, ongoing fight that begins in the assembly area and continues even after the primary objective is secure.

Assembling for Attack

In all types of military operations, including naval and air operations, attacking forces must invariably conduct various preparatory activities prior to an attack. Such activities often involve assembly of forces in specific locations closer to the front or enemy targets, in order to allow for a concentrated and powerful initial offensive blow. The problem is that it is often easy for enemy reconnaissance and intelligence to detect offensive preparations. This makes surprise difficult and emphasizes the importance of the assembly phase.

In general, the quicker and more streamlined the assembly process, the less time the enemy will have to react. When it is impossible to shorten the time needed to assemble forces, it is necessary to attempt to mask friendly intentions through counterintelligence, denial, deception and reconnaissance screens. Another option is to sacrifice a degree of concentration in the attack and have units deploy from more dispersed positions, consolidating en route according to a strict timetable. However, this technique is difficult to execute and can prove vulnerable to enemy counterattack, as units will have trouble fighting cohesively in the opening phases of advance.

It is important to realize that assembly is not only an intelligence contest but also a fight. Once enemy forces identify friendly assembly areas, they may immediately strike with aircraft and artillery in the hopes of disrupting or spoiling the attack. Friendly planners must forecast and prepare responses to these enemy actions, employing counter-battery artillery fire and defensive counter-air assets.

Many elements factor in to this "assembly area battle" that require detailed consideration and planning. For one thing, units may be approaching the assembly area from different distances and along different routes. Some units might arrive at the assembly area later than others. Even if the assembly area is heavily defended, enemy aircraft and artillery might attempt to interdict friendly forces still en route to the assembly area, further complicating the task of preparing for attack.

Thus, leaders must be prepared to fight their way into the assembly area using all available assets, including deception and air defense. The preparation plans or plans for occupying the assembly area must be well choreographed and streamlined, minimizing the time of exposure and giving the enemy the minimum amount of time to react.

Mobility and March Order

Once an operation begins and units depart their assembly areas, the next challenge is the practical and logistical challenge of moving large military forces deep into enemy territory. There are only so many roads and bridges that can support movement of heavy forces. Moving off road can be difficult or impossible depending on weather conditions. If mechanized forces are moving along roads, it can become very difficult to pack a large number of vehicles onto a single road, resulting in long and unwieldy march columns. Moving forces along several parallel roads in close proximity can also prove difficult. Coordinating the movement of multiple columns can be confusing and slow, requiring the use of many phase lines and control measures to prevent units from accidentally shooting each other or moving outside the range of mutual support.

Narrow roads running through restricted terrain such as forests or mountains can prove particularly challenging. Not only does such terrain provide ideal defensive terrain and ambush country for the enemy but it adds additional challenges in keeping the columns moving according to schedule. If a heavy vehicle breaks down or is destroyed by air attack, it might be difficult for recovery vehicles to move past other vehicles in the column to reposition the immobilized vehicle out of the way.

Deployment into Assault Formation

In conventional warfare, terrain will typically dictate where battles will take place. There is a reason so many historical battles have taken place near hills, rivers or cities; these terrain features offer clear advantages to the defender. If a military force has to make a defensive stand, why would it elect to do so in an open field when it could fall back several miles and defend a river crossing? Conversely, by understanding terrain, the attacker can also anticipate the areas of most likely enemy resistance.

Given these principles, when planning an offensive operation, leaders must not only identify a final objective whose capture provides a clear operational or strategic benefit, but must also identify intermediate objectives along the march route that enemy forces have likely occupied. Thus, when moving along a road toward the final objective, offensive planners might identify a key bridge as an intermediate objective, as capture of the bridge will be important to maintaining momentum and speed. Planners might also identify the need to capture a hill that the enemy could use as a strongpoint or observation position, threatening friendly avenues of approach.

In order to be effective in the offense, forces must learn to successfully deploy from approach march formation to assault formation at the appropriate time and place. A unit cannot move long distances while spread out on-line (abreast) in assault formation. It would take too long and the unpredictable effects of rough terrain would make coordinating the movement of multiple columns difficult. Instead, advancing columns move along roads in somewhat densely packed formations that are vulnerable to aircraft and counterattack. Formations can spread out along a road to decrease vulnerability but this will cause march columns to grow longer, reducing the number of forces able to participate in the initial attack or at a minimum making it very difficult for elements near the rear of the column to race to the front in time to respond to enemy contact.

For all the reasons listed above, deploying from march formation into assault formation is a critical combat skill that units should practice frequently. Deploying at precisely the right time and place will give an attacking force a significantly better chance of winning an engagement. Deploying into assault formation on the objective is slightly easier, since the attacking unit knows roughly when and where the deployment will take place and can rehearse beforehand. Deploying to react to chance contact with the enemy is more difficult.

Through detailed terrain and enemy analysis, it is possible to predict the points along the approach route where contact with the enemy is most likely. Leaders can then take steps to prepare for chance contact at those points. Some options include reconnoitering locations in advance with air assets or scout elements, adjusting formation while moving through danger areas, or suppressing suspected enemy positions with indirect fire.

Fighting for the Objective and Sustaining the Advance

The fight for the objective itself and the subsequent logistical challenges of sustaining the advance over time are two of the most complex and challenging aspects of any operation. Defeating a living, thinking enemy on the objective in a highly stressful, chaotic environment demands courage and tactical skill. Given the unpredictability of war and the ever-present factor of human incompetence, it is very possible to win a fight simply thanks to luck or enemy incompetence. Many great battles have been decided entirely in this way.

However, the goal for any unit or leader is to win because of courage and skill, not luck. Earning the victory in this way requires a steadfast dedication to the studies and disciplines laid out so far, as well as a mastery of the tactical level of war, which is beyond the scope of this book. While it is not possible to offer a concise discussion of how to win the tactical battle for the objective, the key point is to recognize how difficult it is to win engagements consistently and the large volume of work and training required to make victory more likely.

The same applies to the extremely complex task of logistics planning and sustaining an advance over an extended period. A detailed discussion of logistics is also beyond the scope of this book but the vital importance of logistics is undeniable. While some leaders have claimed that logistics are more important than tactics, in reality they are very similar disciplines that are of equal importance. Tactics and logistics go hand in hand; neither can prove very effective without the other. While the road to mastery of logistics may not be glamorous or celebrated, victory often hinges on the tireless efforts of military professionals who dedicate themselves to mastering the art of logistics.

Training and Selection

As discussed and demonstrated in the functional model, training and selection is the most critical part of the military machine. This is naturally the case because people, rather than hardware or technology, are the most decisive asset for any combat force. Those people must first be selected and then trained to do their jobs.

No one is born knowing how to do something. Every action taken within a military force had to be trained or learned at some point. Personnel must be trained to do everything from operating advanced weapon systems and sensors, to gathering and analyzing intelligence to providing sustainment services. Those personnel must also be selected to fill their given job, selected for leadership positions or special assignments, and evaluated on their performance. Thus, selection and training permeates every aspect of the military machine.

The following guidelines explain proven scientific methods for training military and security professionals in the most effective way. While in many cases the discussion focuses on conventional military forces preparing for the tactical or physical level of war, this is only for ease of explanation. The same general training and learning principles can apply to any unit or organization, regardless of its operating environment or mission set.

The Four Pillars of Effective Training

The four pillars of an effective training program are proper mindset, situational awareness, skill proficiency and physical fitness. These four pillars might seem overly simple or intuitive, but a deeper understanding of the true nature and interrelation of each of these concepts will highlight their importance.

Proper Mindset

Proper mindset is the most critical of the four pillars. In the simplest terms, military professionals with the proper mindset devote a large volume of time and energy to training for combat and preparing for the worst-case scenario. Combat skills like marksmanship, battlefield communications and tactical medical care decline quickly if units fail to practice them every day. Having the proper mindset means being tough, determined, never cutting corners and taking every precaution to ensure mission success. Units with the proper mindset will set aside time every day to train and maintain weapons systems and personal equipment. In a combat situation, having the proper mindset means being prepared to employ lethal force without hesitation and never quitting during the fight, regardless of fear or pain.

While it is clear that developing the proper mindset is a critical training objective, the precise methods for how to develop the proper mindset are less clear. In the ideal scenario, the proper mindset grows from within, resulting in internally driven, self-motivated individuals. Some units have the luxury of screening for individuals who already possess this drive and self-motivation. Other units possess gifted and inspirational leaders who can build and foster the same self-motivation within their subordinates. In other cases, well-designed training programs and skilled instructors can craft training in a way that enhances the proper mindset and increases each trainee's level of self-motivation.

However, if achieving self-motivation appears difficult or impossible, there are other ways to attempt to improve the mindset of a unit through external motivation and discipline. In some cases, motivation and proper mindset must be hammered into trainees through rigid discipline, rewards and punishments. It is important to remember that if rigid discipline is a soldier's only motivation to do the right thing, it is likely that he/she will falter if challenged to act independently while not under the direct control of superiors.

In other cases, building a team culture that promotes unit pride, camaraderie and even bravado can foster a mindset that will reduce the chances that soldiers will cower in battle. While on the surface bravado may seem hollow, even false bravado has proved almost as effective as real courage in combat situations, since no one wants to appear cowardly in front of his/her comrades. Essentially, units that are not blessed with inspirational leaders or self-motivation must find a way to artificially generate and enforce the proper mindset as much as possible.

Situational Awareness

Lack of situational awareness is one of the leading causes of failure or death in combat. In modern society, most people's situational awareness is very low. They generally spend their day wrapped up in their own thoughts and problems, paying little attention to what is going on around them. People who live in relatively secure environments often fall into even deeper levels of complacency and unpreparedness.

Leaders of combat units must strive to reverse this trend of complacency. Military professionals may have grown up in relatively safe environments, but to survive in the combat zone they must nurture their innate survival instincts.

People with the proper mindset described earlier understand the importance of situational awareness and make disciplined efforts to cultivate it. Situational awareness begins with the awareness of threats and awareness that the worst-case scenario is always a possibility. Situational awareness also involves keeping up to date with intelligence reports, studying enemy tactics, and developing a deep regional and cultural expertise on the theater of operations. Situational awareness calls for an effort to remain alert at all times without being paranoid.

The core attribute of situational awareness has many indirect applications as well. Situational awareness includes being aware of faults or dysfunction within a unit, and understanding friendly and enemy strengths and weaknesses. It also entails recognizing if training or reform efforts are proving effective or ineffective. Situational awareness also helps predict and identify unintended outcomes of decisions and combat actions, including second- and third-order effects.

Skill Proficiency

After cultivating the proper mindset and maintaining good situational awareness, the next step is to develop the proper skills or tools required to prevail in a real combat situation. When striving to improve skill proficiency, it is important to choose sound techniques that are simple, effective, easy to perform and can realistically apply to a real-life scenario. After identifying the best techniques, the next step is to practice and rehearse them repeatedly until they become second nature. This will maximize the chances of rapid and appropriate response in a high-stress situation.

Skill proficiency does not apply only to the individual soldier. Just as a soldier can practice changing magazines or setting up a machine gun, planning staffs can practice designing and briefing operational concepts. Intelligence analysts can practice their language skills and broaden their knowledge about threats and theaters of war. Leaders can work to improve their charisma and the interpersonal skills required to inspire and lead troops. Every military profession includes a set of skills that are essential for achieving success. It is the job of a true professional to devote tireless effort to mastering those skills.

Physical Fitness

Even skilled fighters with the proper mindset and high levels of situational awareness can lose a fight simply because they run out of energy. To maintain adequate levels of combat fitness, it is not necessary to achieve the same fitness level as a professional or Olympic athlete. Rather, the key is to stay healthy and maintain decent levels of cardiovascular endurance, running speed, functional strength and coordination. Popular commercial fitness programs don't always focus on the most useful abilities needed for combat. Many people jog, but how many also run sprints to build speed? Simply being able to run fast without falling is one of the most critical survival skills in a gunfight or emergency situation, yet people rarely practice sprinting.

Physical fitness is not just about running fast or lifting heavy weights. Physical fitness provides the capacity to train. The previous pillar, skill proficiency, demands a certain volume of work. Trainees who do not have the endurance or physical ability to achieve the adequate volume will not progress. This principle applies to any kind of training. If it takes 4 hours of daily practice to improve at the violin, a student must first develop the finger strength to play for four hours.

Physical fitness is also important for moral or psychological reasons. Units with high standards for physical fitness, that take pride in maintaining their health and physical professionalism, typically prove more cohesive and effective than units with lower standards. In conventional units, the same can even apply to neatness of dress and military bearing. An inward focus and outward display of professionalism has a positive psychological effect on the unit as a whole. Taking pride in physical fitness and a healthy lifestyle is a key goal for a professional military unit.

Conversely, it is possible for units to be too focused on physical fitness and neglect other critical aspects of the military profession. While physical fitness is essential, it is not necessarily the most important attribute for every profession. For example, while it is helpful for tank gunners to be fit, it is more important for them to be able to shoot accurately and destroy enemy tanks on the battlefield. It is also important not to discount the potential contributions of military professionals who are less fit. If an intelligence analyst is less physically fit, that might not be ideal, but it does not affect his/her ability to do brilliant analytical work. The best units find a balance, encouraging all unit members to strive for excellent fitness, regardless of their profession, while recognizing that other attributes besides fitness are important too.

Mastering the Basics

As discussed earlier, in combat, the unexpected is inevitable. In the U.S. military, unexpected bad luck is sometimes referred to as "Murphy." When a poorly trained unit is engaged in combat and Murphy shows up, the unit can only devote 10 percent of its attention to Murphy because the remaining 90 percent is consumed by basic tasks like how to change magazines, how to select covered and concealed firing positions, and how to call for indirect fire. Essentially, in a high-stress situation, a poorly trained unit immediately becomes inwardly focused on process instead of outwardly focused on the problem and the enemy. Such a unit won't last long against an elite opponent and must be lucky to win.

The main thing that sets an elite unit apart is that it can focus almost all of its attention on Murphy because the basics are taking care of themselves. An elite unit has mastered the basics to the point that they are automatic and second nature. This allows for outward focus on the problem and the enemy. It also allows for learning and improvement in the higher-level combat arts. Developing "game sense" and the capacity for pattern recognition first requires that the soldier is able to see the pattern. If a soldier spends every engagement focused on fumbling through magazine changes, he/she is missing the learning opportunity for how to maneuver and fight.

Many scholars have conducted studies showing that achieving this level of skill or expertise requires something approaching twenty years of experience. This is simply not true. The fact is that all of us achieve expertise in various skills in a far shorter time. Most of us, for example, are experts in driving a car. If a deer jumps in front of us on the highway, our foot goes to the brake and our hands manipulate the wheel before we even know what we are doing. If the deer jumps from the right, we turn the wheel left. If the deer jumps from the left, we turn the wheel right. Our action is not just a spontaneous conditioned response that happens the same way every time; rather, it is a spontaneous creative action that can be different every time depending on the situation. Without this spontaneous creative action, we have to consciously think about what we are doing and we will hit the deer.

Noel Burch's Four Stages of Learning

When we are learning to drive we pass through four stages: unconscious incompetence, conscious incompetence, conscious competence and unconscious competence.[30] Military units pass through the same stages on the road to mastery.

The first stage is unconscious incompetence, where we don't know what we don't know. This is comparable to the young child who is certain he/she could drive a car if only given the chance. Understandably, this stage is the most dangerous and can result in unpleasant surprises.

The second stage is conscious incompetence, where we at least know what we don't know. This is the stage where we might have jerked around a parking lot with our parents, unable to make the car do what we wanted it to. However, after continued practice, our parents agreed that we had reached the level of conscious competence, and they tell us we can drive into town by ourselves for the first time. Our hearts raced as we walked to the car, then we carefully drove into town, having to maintain an unbroken concentration on the task at hand. This is an example of conscious competence.

Finally, many of us today can drive while talking on the phone, fiddling with the radio, eating, or doing any number of things. If a deer jumps in front of our car while we are changing the station, we will still react spontaneously and unconsciously. This unconscious competence is another term for spontaneous creative action.

Spontaneous Creative Action vs. Conditioned Response

The distinction between these two concepts is absolutely critical for effective training. What sets spontaneous creative action apart from simple conditioned response is that it can adapt to changing circumstances. A pianist can train to play the same song the same way every time, with no conscious thought. If asked to change the song in certain places, the pianist will have difficulty, as he/she will instinctively revert to playing the piece in the rehearsed way. Training for conditioned response means that an action or task will be performed exactly the same way every time.

On a number of occasions, conditioned response has proven extremely dangerous. On one occasion, a police officer and martial arts practitioner swiftly grabbed a gun from an assailant and then gave it right back. Luckily, the officer's partner arrived in time to resolve the situation.[31] Why did the officer give the gun back to the assailant? Because that's how he had practiced the movement in the dojo countless times, giving the gun back to his opponent after each repetition.

Given this example, conditioned response is obviously not the goal. How do we teach ourselves to adapt and act creatively faster than we can think? While it is possible to achieve mastery of a simple skill like driving a car merely by driving every day, mastering more complex combat skills with more variables requires a slightly more refined process. In truth, drivers go through this process when learning to drive without even realizing it.

Repetitive Drill

The path to mastery proceeds through three steps: repetitive drill, variable patterns, and competitive scenarios. If trainees skip any one of these steps or fail to achieve mastery in one phase before proceeding to the next, they will most likely fail in combat. The first phase, repetitive drill, allows the trainee to encode certain movements or processes in the brain so they become instinctive or second nature.

In order for drills to be useful, they first must be the right size. Drills that are too big restrict adaptability. Drills that are too small reduce speed. For example, some of the U.S. Army's battle drills are likely too big because they apply a rigid formula to a rather complex action, such as engaging an enemy force and maneuvering for a flank assault.

To better understand this concept, consider an analogy. A house builder goes to a lumberyard and asks for materials to build a house. The lumber merchant offers the builder a variety of prefabricated house parts such as an exterior wall that is 20 feet by 10 feet. The builder says these prefabricated parts do not necessarily match his vision for the house. What if he wants his wall to be 25 feet by 10 feet? He asks the lumber merchant for materials that offer more flexibility. The merchant turns and points to the forest outside, assuring the builder that he can cut the trees in any size he wants. The builder is frustrated, asking if there isn't some "happy medium" that allows for flexible design without the burden of chopping down trees.

In fact, the kind of lumber typically offered in stores fits this description exactly. Over the years, people realized that there were certain cuts of lumber such as 2x4s and 4x4s that could be prefabricated but then combined and arranged in infinite combinations. These cuts of wood are not too big and not too small. They are just right to allow for maximum convenience (speed) while providing complete flexibility. A training drill must fit this same description.

A good rule of thumb for determining the size of a drill is that it should be something that always needs to be done the same way. For example, barring debilitating physical injury, we always change our magazine in the same way. There is no creative way to change magazines and there would be no benefit to doing it different ways each time. In small unit tactics, while a complex battle drill involving multiple maneuvering elements is too big, a simple immediate action drill is just the right size. In such a drill, a small unit will seek cover, return fire, come on-line and report the distance, direction and description of the enemy contact. This is a drill that can be performed the same way every time and must happen so fast that there will be no benefit to variation.

Whether a drill is for an individual or for a unit, the method of drill training remains the same. The key is maximum number of repetitions. If a unit only practices a drill one hundred times, it will have little hope of instinctively executing the drill in a high-stress combat situation. While some scholars suggest there is a magic number to achieve mastery, the better solution is simply to continue repetition and test for mastery. It will usually take several thousand repetitions over the course of several sleep cycles, because the motor cortex encodes motor programs during sleep. It is easier to conceptualize this drill mastery process if we follow the following steps:

1. Perform the drill slowly, focusing on details and ensuring that form is correct and there are no mistakes.
2. Increase speed and use a time standard (stopwatch) to push for faster and faster times.

3. Incorporate distraction in the form of a blindfold, darkness, noise, etc. and continue practicing until the drill can be performed with distraction almost as fast as it can be performed without distraction.
4. Test for internalization by forcing trainees to execute the drill without warning or while the conscious mind is occupied with something else. Any hesitation or stuttering means mastery has not been achieved. The trainee must be able to react instantaneously and seamlessly.

Once a drill is mastered it can sometimes be useful to move on to other drills that overlap or interfere with the encoded behavior. A good trainer has developed a sequence of drills that the student will practice in sequence. Often it is useful to ensure a student fully masters one drill before proceeding to the next. This maximizes the interference effect caused by learning the next drill if the two drills overlap at certain points. This would be akin to telling a piano player to learn to play a song flawlessly, then changing certain parts of the song and challenging the player to be able to instantly transition between both versions. This kind of training helps break down rigid, conditioned response and foster a more flexible spontaneous creative action.

VARIABLE PATTERNS

The real transition to spontaneous creative action comes in the next step: variable patterns. This forces the trainee to put drills together in different combinations. Drills are the building blocks, the metaphorical 2x4s and 4x4s of combat training. Variable patterns are about learning to nail those pieces of wood together in different combinations. For example, in training a soldier to shoot, a variable pattern for combat marksmanship might include the following tasks:

1. Sprint to the first barrier and fire two shots from the kneeling position to the left 100m target and two shots to the right 100m target.
2. Switch to the prone position and fire four shots to the 200m target.
3. Combat reload and sprint to the first window; fire two shots from the standing position at each of three steel targets.
4. Transition to the pistol, sprint to the next window and fire from the standing position to knock down four "pepper-popper" targets.

The trainee (or the whole unit) will run through this pattern over and over, timing each iteration and competing for a faster time. Then the instructor will change the pattern. There are some patterns with proven value (like the El Presidente drill) that may be practiced over and over in multiple training sessions. These prepackaged combinations are good for use as a performance benchmark over time and save the instructor having to explain every drill.

Variable patterns do not only apply to tactical shooting. The same variable pattern principle can be used to train all basic combat arms skills. One example is the "immediate action drill" already mentioned, in which soldiers take cover, return fire, come on-line and report. That is a drill. To incorporate this drill into a variable pattern, a small unit leader might walk his/her element in formation through the woods and randomly call out, "Contact left! Contact front! Contact rear!" The element will practice this immediate action over and over for hours every day. Then the leader might incorporate things like bounding, indirect fire, and machine gun employment to form different patterns.

Another useful thing about variable patterns is that they force trainees to react to their environment. For example, practicing the kind of four-way react to contact drill described above really becomes useful when it is performed on various types of terrain. A common novice mistake is to fail to find covered and concealed firing positions. Green soldiers performing the drill will find themselves lying in the open or hiding behind one-inch-thick trees that would never protect them in combat. Pattern training teaches the mind to be always "switched-on" and subconsciously looking for the next covered and concealed position. When soldiers practice reacting to contact from all directions while moving through woods and varied terrain, they eventually learn to find good covered and concealed firing positions without thinking.

COMPETITIVE SCENARIOS

Repetitive drills and variable patterns are of only marginal value if trainees do not have the opportunity to engage in real, free-play competition. While variable patterns in particular help break rigidity and improve spontaneity, the true test of spontaneous creative action is being able to react to a living, thinking opponent.

Scripted scenarios are not nearly as useful as free-play scenarios. It is possible to succeed in a scripted scenario by following a rigid checklist or sequence of procedures. However, learning to place faith in a procedural approach can be catastrophic in combat. To understand the importance of competition, it is useful to tell a story. During a debate between military officers, some of the officers claimed that checklists and rigid processes were useful in combat while others claimed they were not. The anti-checklist group claimed that checklists could not work in an environment with many changing variables. The pro-checklist group retorted by providing an example of a pilot who used a checklist to land a plane in a raging storm. Certainly, the pilot had to deal with a myriad of changing variables, but the checklist brought him down safely.

In truth, both groups completely missed the true nature of the problem of combat. What makes checklists problematic is not the presence of variables but rather the competitive nature of combat. There is a big difference between combat and landing a plane in a storm. When the pilot compensates for a crosswind by using the rudder, the wind doesn't respond by thinking, "he's pushing his rudder to the left...I'm going to switch direction to flip him over and smash him into the ground." The biggest problem in combat is not random variables but rather the living, thinking opponent who is consciously trying to subvert friendly actions and destroy friendly forces.

It is impossible to use a checklist to win a chess game or any other game. The best chess players have played so many games against so many opponents that they develop an uncanny ability for pattern recognition. A chess master can see many moves ahead and can even read a new opponent's intentions based on behavior cues. Great competitors have a real "game sense" that comes only from repeated exposure to real life opponents. It is impossible to develop game sense by running through scripted scenarios, no matter how realistic or varied they are.

In addition to being free-play competitions, scenarios should be as realistic as possible. The closer a scenario comes to the real thing, the better prepared soldiers will be when they engage in real combat. It is also important to remember that number of iterations is particularly important in scenario training, as it is in the preceding phases as well. Some military units might conduct one or two realistic free-play scenarios per year. This is obviously inadequate. Using the training methods and techniques discussed later in this section, it is possible to do two or more scenarios each day.

Another common error is that some units run scenarios before they have mastered drills and variable patterns. Even a well-crafted scenario will prove less useful for a unit that has not mastered the basics to the point that they are second nature and practiced performing those basic tasks in different patterns and combinations. This would be like telling someone who had never boxed before to get into the ring with a champion. All the novice would learn would be how to get pounded. Worse, the experience might teach the novice to expect to lose, reduce confidence, and encourage timidity or caution in future engagements. It is best to send trainees into a scenario armed with enough tools to give them a fighting chance.

Multimedia Sequencing

In addition to the progression from repetitive drill to variable patterns to competitive scenarios, it is also useful for trainees to make multiple passes over the same material using different learning methods and media. There are specific rules of thumb for the sequence of activities that can improve the quality and speed of learning. What follows is one example of how to sequence a training course in a given subject such as urban warfare.

1. **Start with a shock scenario:** This is the only time when it is a good idea to throw trainees into the ring knowing they are probably going to fail catastrophically. As soon as trainees show up, without warning, launch them into a realistic scenario. It could be a field exercise, computer simulation or tactical decision game (TDG). It should be high-stress and relatively short. It should also not be overly dangerous, since lack of experience will increase the chance of accidents. When the trainees inevitably perform poorly in the scenario, it will accomplish three things. First, it will provide context for the training that follows. Second, it will lower ego-based barriers to learning by reminding trainees that they do in fact need the training. Third, it will provide instructors with a quick evaluation that will allow them to identify and focus on key areas of weakness.

2. **Video homework:** It is often a good idea to break up training subjects with a sleep cycle. For example, instead of doing single rooms on Monday and hallways on Tuesday, it is better to do an introduction or shock scenario for single rooms on Monday night, then send the trainees home to sleep on it (with homework), then bring them back to finish single rooms on

Tuesday morning and introduce hallways Tuesday night. This gives trainees time to absorb and digest each lesson. Videos are good for homework assignments after a shock scenario. Videos are often easier to absorb than readings and are impossible to skim or rush through. The videos should be relatively short, no more than an hour. In this case, the video would review concepts the students experienced in the shock scenario and familiarize them with the subjects to be taught the next day.

3. Pop quiz: This determines that all the students watched the video. There are many ways to conduct a pop quiz, but one of the best and easiest is for the instructor to hand out blank sheets of paper and present a simple tactical problem on the board, designed so that anyone who watched the video could solve it. The trainees have a limited time to draw out their solution on the blank paper and write their name on the top. Then trainees trade their solutions amongst each other. Now trainees are instructed to correct mistakes on their peers' papers and to put their name at the bottom. The instructor goes around the room, quizzing trainees on their solutions and looking for mistakes. As necessary, the instructor will examine the sheets of paper, evaluating trainees not only on their answers but also on their ability to correct the mistakes of others. Anyone suspected of not doing the homework is grilled and questioned in front of the group. The intensity and nature of this grilling depends on the nature of the training and the authority of the instructor. However, it is critical that trainees take the work seriously and never blow off assignments.

4. Classroom presentation: Once the quiz is complete, trainees receive a presentation or class. The experience of the shock exercise, video and quiz will provide good material for discussion and learning. Instructors should avoid long, dry presentations that put the trainees to sleep. Instead, the class should be an active, challenging discussion with lots of questions and practical examples.

5. Tabletop drills: After receiving the class, trainees break into groups and practice executing what they learned, using tabletop maps or blueprints. The instructor will ask a trainee how to clear a certain type of room or configuration and the trainee will show the answer, moving small pieces on the board. The trainee must explain what he/she is doing while moving the pieces, without hesitating or stuttering. After the trainee is complete, the instructor asks the rest of the group for critiques. The trainees repeat these drills over and over until they can run though any configuration without mistakes, hesitation or stuttering. It is very important that the trainees move the pieces smoothly and decisively, without jittery indecision. It is also critical that trainees articulate everything they are doing in clear, confident speech.

6. Marked ground training: After completing numerous repetitions using the tabletop drills, the trainees will move outside and practice the same movements and configurations, moving through notional buildings created with stakes and engineer tape. They will repeat these movements over and over until they can do them quickly and smoothly with no mistakes.

7. Tabletop scenarios: The trainees then return to the tabletop; however, this time the instructor will randomly change the configuration of rooms and obstacles while the trainee is moving the pieces. For example, the trainee might start clearing a hallway and the instructor might drop a refrigerator or soda machine into the hallway while the trainee is talking. The instructor might add or remove doors or danger areas unexpectedly. The trainee must seamlessly adjust the approach without hesitating or stuttering. Again, when each trainee finishes an iteration, the other trainees provide critiques. The critique process is critical for keeping all trainees engaged in the exercise and keeping the mind active.

8. Computer simulation force-on-force: Trainees now go home and square off against each other in urban warfare, using multiplayer online computer simulations.

9. Shoot house paper-target runs: After the computer simulation homework, trainees move to the shoot house and conduct multiple runs, firing nonlethal projectiles at paper targets. The instructor will move targets around between iterations. After each iteration the instructor conducts an after-action review (AAR), compiling a record of lessons learned during the exercise.

10. Shoot house force-on-force: After the nonlethal paper target runs, the trainees conduct force-on-force with nonlethal projectiles. To begin, the instructor places limitations on the opposing force, then eventually lets them come up with their own cunning plans to win the engagement. After each iteration the instructor conducts an AAR, compiling a record of lessons learned during the exercise.

11. Shoot house live-fire or stress runs: At this point, the goal is to raise the stress level to the maximum through the use of live bullets, stressors or both. Examples of stressors include loud pneumatic guns, loudspeakers, flashbangs, flashing lights, darkness, smoke, etc.

12. Training manual reading assignment: Traditional textbook/manual reading assignments are best used as a follow-up and review of the practical exercises. The reading assignment should be as in-depth and detailed as possible, illuminating theory as well as practice and reinforcing concepts with stories and historical examples.

13. Written test: A simple written test is a good way to verify completion of the reading assignment and provide a comprehensive review of all subjects covered during training.

14. Sustainment: The most important reason for the manual is to offer a reference for trainees to sustain their knowledge. In addition to the manual, trainees should have video references, flashcards, smart cards, audio manuals, and audio versions of the training videos to listen to in the car, while running or while doing chores around the house, etc. Trainees should also have continued access to computer simulations where they can square off against each other, over and over again.

15. High stress evaluation: Ideally, it is best not to conduct the evaluation immediately after the trainees finish a particular subject, as a good evaluation tests sustainment as well as learning. Evaluations should always be a surprise with no warning beforehand of the timing or subjects of evaluations. Thus, if trainees finish the urban warfare module and have spent three weeks practicing rural operations, then is the time to unexpectedly test their urban warfare ability. Evaluations can employ any of the techniques described so far but should focus on realistic field exercises, as close to real combat as possible. Surprise tests will force trainees to review their knowledge constantly and keep their skills sharp.

The multimedia sequence described above is by no means a rigid formula that must be followed. Instructors might want to leave out certain activities or conduct them in a different order. The important thing is to achieve the maximum number of iterations and to go over the same thing many times in different ways. Every trainee's learning style is different. It is impractical for the instructor to tailor the teaching methodology to fit each trainee's learning style; therefore, it is good to flood the trainees with all types of learning: written, game, video, audio, practical, etc. Multiple iterations across the multimedia spectrum are much more useful than dry repetition using the same teaching method or media repeatedly.

Some media, such as the tabletop, provide additional benefits in speed, cost and efficiency. For example, to conduct a full-blown patrol including movement to the objective, recon of the objective rally point, occupying the objective rally point, recon of the objective, actions on the objective, consolidation and reorganization can take an entire day in the field, and only one trainee will get the opportunity to lead a patrol that day. Using the tabletop, trainees can run through an entire patrol in a matter of minutes while other trainees observe and look for mistakes. In just a few hours, every trainee can complete dozens of iterations in the leadership position. This allows trainees to hit the ground running when they get to the field, and helps cut costs for certain resource-intensive field exercises.

Prioritization and Tracking

Many units spend a lot of time developing mission essential task lists (METL) and using them to ensure that the training priorities of each level of command are "nested" or focused toward the same goals. This is obviously very important, but some units spend more time worrying about crafting the METL than they do actually training. Furthermore, after all that analysis, the results are often obvious and were apparent on the surface from the beginning. For example, when conducting counterinsurgency in Iraq, it is not necessary to analyze mission essential task lists from the division downward to figure out that a platoon needs to practice reacting to an IED attack. Conversely, after days or weeks of overcomplicated

METL analysis, it is possible to overlook something as obvious as learning to react to an IED attack.

Whatever system a unit chooses to use, complex or simple, the important part is that units up and down the chain of command maintain good communication, align their priorities and focus training on the highest priority areas first, based on intelligence and enemy pattern analysis. There are countless practical ways to do this that many units overlook. For example, if a unit knows it will be relieving another unit that is currently overseas, those two units should talk every day to synchronize stateside training with the reality in the combat zone.

In addition to prioritization, tracking training and sustainment is critical. Each unit should have a training matrix showing the last time it conducted any given drill, pattern or type of exercise. Ideally, the matrix should include the actual performance or times achieved by each soldier, crew or unit. There should be a constant competition to achieve the best scores and best times, and winners should be rewarded and recognized.

For example, assembly/disassembly of a machine gun is a simple drill every soldier in the unit must master. The unit standard must be completion of the task in a given par time while blindfolded. The matrix should show and confirm that every soldier in the unit has practiced numerous times and met the standard. The matrix should also show each soldier's best times in each drill or event.

For larger exercises and competitive scenarios, each one should produce a detailed after-action review (AAR). Those AARs should be analyzed, disseminated and compiled in frequently updated "living documents" that can be used to drive training and evaluate readiness. Most importantly, AAR comments and insights should be shared between units both horizontally and vertically. Not only will this help improve training but it also will create a habit of sharing lessons learned that will carry over onto the battlefield.

Common Indicators of Poor Training

1. How many actual repetitions or iterations does each trainee perform? Whatever the training task might be, from assembling a machine gun, calling for indirect fire or leading a patrol, how many times does each trainee get to run through the process? Running through once or twice is entirely useless. For some physical activities, even one hundred iterations are of limited value. If training does not focus on letting trainees actually do the task over and over, it is not good training.

2. Does the unit conduct after-action reviews and disseminate the results? Trainees and instructors should both constantly evaluate their performance and record lessons learned to improve for next time. Leaders should be able to walk up to any instructor or student and ask to see the AAR from the previous day's training. If no one can produce the AAR, there is a potential dysfunction. More importantly, units should share AAR results up the chain, down the chain, and with their fellow units to the left and right. Sharing AAR results is the best indicator that they are not thoughtlessly or hastily compiled. In some cases, a unit will conduct or record an AAR simply because it is a requirement but put little thought or effort into it and never take the time to study or review the AAR later on. A unit would not bother to share such an AAR, so the fact that a unit shares an AAR is also an indicator that the AAR was well done.

3. Do instructors know their trainees? Instructors should be able to articulate who are the strong trainees in the class and who are weak. More importantly, the instructor should be able to cite from memory the particular strengths and weaknesses of each trainee. If the instructor cannot cite this information from memory, it should be physically written down somewhere in an organized format. Great instructors go as far as bringing home tapes of trainees and watching them over and over, taking notes on what to help each student with the next day.

4. Does training focus on combat, adaptability, and worst-case scenarios? If instructors spend many hours teaching patrolling, going through how to move in the woods, how to set up an objective rally point or how to send out a recon, the training is almost useless if they do not spend at least equal time practicing what happens if the unit is attacked during any one of those processes. The whole reason there is a specific way to recon and set up an objective rally point is to protect the unit from attack. Thus, once trainees know the mechanics or drills of patrolling, the next step is to have them respond to attacks from any direction at any point in the patrol. What happens if the recon gets hit on the way back to the objective rally point? What happens if the recon takes casualties? What happens if the objective rally point takes indirect fire while the main element is on the objective? If training does not focus on these kinds of scenarios with unexpected variables over and over, a unit will likely panic when it must deal with these problems for the first time.

5. Does training incorporate a living and thinking opponent? If the good guys always win and the OPFOR (opposing force) moves are scripted, the training is of limited value. Training must at the very least include free play force-on-force scenarios where the OPFOR can win.

6. Are scenarios predictable? A common example is a unit practicing a react-to-contact drill many times, but only with an enemy attack from the front. Good training will include attacks from the right, left, rear, and multiple directions simultaneously or sequentially. Scenarios must incorporate stress and new, unexpected variables.

7. Are trainees held accountable for mistakes? In an effective training evolution, instructors will point out numerous mistakes on each iteration, write them down, and force students to repeat the drills, patterns or scenarios over and over until the mistakes are corrected. A course where the instructor simply pats trainees on the back and moves on to the next exercise is either much too easy or poorly executed.

8. Are trainees ever sitting around during training? Trainees should never be idle during training. Even if they are waiting for their turn to perform an activity, they should be practicing something, going over notes, quizzing each other, etc. Instructors should be on top of the trainees all the time, correcting anyone who is not focused on training, quizzing trainees unexpectedly, and punishing them for incorrect answers. Obviously, in more elite units punishments might not be needed.

9. Can students fail the course? If no one fails the course, it is obviously not very difficult and is therefore of limited value. If instructors claim that the purpose of the course is simply to pass on knowledge, that is an irrational excuse. How do instructors know the knowledge is passed on if they do not conduct challenging evaluations? If no one fails those evaluations, they are not difficult enough. In specialized or volunteer units, those who fail can be cut. In conventional units, those who fail should be retrained or recycled in the course. Attrition in any course should be at least 20 percent. This does not necessarily mean that students need to "fail" the course and not graduate. Rather, students should simply fail to meet course standards at least 20 percent of the time, "training at the edge of failure." Retraining or recycling through training is always an option when students fail to meet course standards.

10. Do instructors emphasize sustainment? If instructors do not have a specific and detailed plan for how students are going to sustain the skills gained in a course, and if they do not pass that plan on to students, the course is of limited value. Leaders should be able to ask any instructor or any student the plan for sustaining the knowledge gained in the course. If there is no specific and detailed answer to this question, there is a potential dysfunction.

11. Do instructors have written course materials and do they provide materials to the students? Except in some rare cases where secrecy is an issue, instructors should have many professional manuals and references to support training. Instructors should also provide trainees with take-home materials to aid in retention and sustainment of the topics covered. If there is no written documentation to back up the lessons of the course, it is difficult to standardize or maintain combat capabilities.

12. Are trainees falling asleep? Even if trainees are not literally falling asleep, if the instructor is talking and unaware that no one is listening, the training is probably of limited value. Any course that calls for an instructor to just talk at students for long hours without any kind of engagement, feedback or practical exercise is rarely effective.

13. Are trainees asking questions? This is one of the best indicators of course effectiveness. If students are not asking questions, instructors must assume the training is not engaging the students' minds and take action to get the students more involved in the learning process.

14. What is the quality and background of the instructors? At a minimum, instructors must be highly skilled and able to demonstrate mastery of the subject matter they are teaching. Ideally, instructors should also possess personal experience in real-world combat scenarios. Not only will a skilled instructor do a better job of planning and conducting training, but high levels of experience and professionalism also motivate students to take training seriously and give maximum effort.

SELECTION

Selection is one of the most critical factors influencing the performance enhancement equation. An organization's methods of selecting individuals for promotion and units for key assignments incentivizes certain traits or attributes and encourages their growth within the organization. If an organization promotes individuals primarily based on their physical fitness, everyone in the organization will focus on improving fitness levels in order to secure promotion and may neglect other areas because there is no incentive to focus on them.

This phenomenon of incentives is a double-edged sword. In some cases, selection or promotion systems unknowingly incentivize the wrong attributes. For example, consider a promotion system where the most important factor for promotion is a favorable written evaluation from superiors. While it might seem logical that a superior officer is best qualified to evaluate his/her subordinates and a superior's opinion should carry the most weight, there may be unintended side effects associated with this approach.

If the most important factor for promotion is a positive evaluation from superiors, every member of the organization will focus on pleasing his/her superiors and neglect other things. In such a system, earning the respect of subordinates and peers might have no effect on an individual's prospect for promotion. This will encourage leaders to neglect subordinates and clash with peers to win the favor of superiors, breeding a culture of sycophants and "yes-men." To make matters worse, if yes-men are promoted in front of others, they will rise to positions where they can have greater influence on the force as a whole. Conversely, leaders who are not yes-men may grow frustrated and leave the force early. Thus, incentivizing a certain trait slowly spreads that trait to the entire force and drives out those who do not possess it.

Understanding the power of incentives makes it clear how important it is to incentivize the right attributes instead of the wrong ones. This is actually easier to accomplish than it appears. All it requires is to identify the traits that will actually lead to success and mission accomplishment in the real world. At the most basic level, the mission of any military force is simple: win the fight. Therefore, the logical next step is to incentivize winning. Is the ability to put on a show for superiors helpful for winning on the battlefield? Most likely it is not, so it makes no sense to incentivize that ability. What if instead a unit conducts frequent and realistic force-on-force training exercises or competitions, and the leaders who win most often are promoted? This approach incentivizes winning; instead of spending time trying to please superiors, leaders will spend time training hard to win the next fight.

Some might argue that existing promotion systems based on a superior's evaluation already accomplish this in a different way. The argument would be that superiors account for factors such as performance in training exercises and leadership ability when writing their evaluations. In some cases this might indeed be true; however, in other cases it might not, and there is no sure way to tell the difference. Does a glowing evaluation truly reflect a leader's abilities or is it simply the result of favoritism? It is impossible to know.

In reality, if the actual factor that triggers promotion is the evaluation of a superior, that is most likely what people will focus on, rather than focusing on performance in the hope that superiors will recognize and appreciate it. It is more practical to directly incentivize the skills and attributes inherent in victory. Even quantifiable performance measures will offer much better results. For example, many Cold War armor units focused on subordinate units' tank gunnery scores when considering the commanders of those units for promotion. While accurate shooting is not the only skill required for tanks to win in combat, it is certainly an important one.

Cold War armor units that incentivized gunnery generally saw very positive results. Units and crews would fight with each other over limited simulator time, trying to squeeze in as much practice as possible to improve scores. This is proof that incentives clearly work. The next step is to incentivize more skills and traits that are useful in combat and place less emphasis on traits that do not promote mission success. This will create a chain reaction. Promoting individuals who possess the right attributes to win the fight will eventually result in the majority of command positions across the force being filled with fighters and winners.

Conclusion

The goal of this book is to encourage thinking, rather than provide solutions. History shows that efforts to find definitive solutions or fixed principles in combat frequently prove misguided. In the end, no checklist, no book and no system can actually win the fight. That vitally important mission falls on the shoulders of human beings who must use their brains to solve complex and ambiguous problems in high-stress environments.

The scope of this book does not allow for a comprehensive survey of modern warfare, combat training and performance. Though the concepts are universal, most of the analysis merely scratches the surface of important issues. Yet, if this book inspires even one military, law-enforcement or security professional to think deeply about how to improve his/her combat performance, we have achieved our objective.

The contemporary security environment is evolving rapidly and growing increasingly complex. It is vitally important to focus on decisions and reforms that have the greatest positive effect on the chances of success in future conflict. The basic starting point for such decisions and reforms is combat performance enhancement. The first step along the path to victory is empowering the brave men and women who serve the cause of freedom to enhance their performance and achieve their maximum potential.

Notes

[1] Michael R. Gordon and General Bernard E. Trainor, *The Endgame: The Inside Story of the Struggle for Iraq, from George W. Bush to Barack Obama* (New York: Vintage Books 2012), Kindle locations 737, 1201 and 3115.

[2] Anthony Cordesman, *The Iraq War: Strategy, Tactics, and Military Lessons* (Washington DC: CSIS Press 2003), pp. 304-310.

[3] Mark S. Bennett, "Border Security: One Step Toward Resolving the Conflict in Iraq," Air Command and Staff College Paper, p. 10.

[4] Derek Trunkey, "Implications of the Department of Defense Readiness Reporting System," Congressional Budget Office May 2013, p. 1; "Linking the Readiness of Armed Forces to DoD's Operation and Maintenance Spending," Congressional Budget Office April 2011, p. 12; Harrison, Todd, "Rethinking Readiness," Strategic Studies Quarterly, Fall 2014, p. 55.

[5] Peter Paret, *Makers of Modern Strategy from Machiavelli to the Nuclear Age* (Princeton: Princeton University Press 2010), p. 296.

[6] Daniel J. Hughes and Harry Bell, *Moltke on the Art of War: Selected Writings* (New York: Ballantine 2009), p. 92.

[7] Carl von Clausewitz, *On War* (Princeton: Princeton University Press 2008), p. 119.

[8] Militärgeschichtliches Forschungsamt, *Germany and the Second World War Vol. II*, (Oxford: Oxford University Press 1996), p. 254

[9] John Toland, *The Rising Sun: The Decline and Fall of the Japanese Empire 1936-1945* (New York: Random House 2014), Kindle location 1230.

[10] Barry Posen, *The Sources of Military Doctrine: France, Britain, and Germany between the World Wars* (Ithaca: Cornell University Press 2014), p. 1.

[11] Timothy Lupfer, *The Dynamics Of Doctrine: The Changes In German Tactical Doctrine During The First World War* (Pickle Partners Publishing 2014), Kindle location 96.

[12] Arthur Collins, *Common Sense Training: A Working Philosophy for Leaders* (New York: Random House 2011), Kindle location 3252.

[13] Walter Kretchik, *U.S. Army Doctrine: From the American Revolution to the War on Terror* (Lawrence: University Press of Kansas 2014), Kindle location 5636.

[14] William S. Lind, *Maneuver Warfare Handbook* (Boulder: Westview Press 1985), Kindle location 173.

[15] Williamson Murray, *Military Innovation in the Interwar Period* (Cambridge: Cambridge University Press 1996), p. 41.

[16] Jack Snyder, *The Ideology of the Offensive: Military Decision Making and the Disasters of 1914* (Ithaca: Cornell University Press 2013), Kindle location 200.

[17] Harry Summers, *On Strategy: A Critical Analysis of the Vietnam War* (New York: Random House 2009), Kindle location 125.

[18] Wayne Hughes, *Fleet Tactics and Coastal Combat* (Annapolis: Naval Institute Press 2014), Kindle location 343.

[19] Bernard Law Montgomery, *The Memoirs of Field Marshal Montgomery* (Barnsley: Pen & Sword 2012), Kindle Location 1483.

[20] Michael Howard, "The Use of Military History," The Causes of Wars and Other Essays (Cambridge: Harvard University Press 1983), p. 194.

[21] John Nagl, *Learning to Eat Soup with a Knife: Counterinsurgency Lessons from Malaya and Vietnam* (Chicago: University of Chicago Press 2005), Kindle Location 3006.

[22] Ibid., Kindle Location 68.
[23] Robert Komer, *The Malayan Emergency in Retrospect: Organization of a Successful Counterinsurgency Effort* (Santa Monica: RAND 1972), p. v.
[24] Robert Taber, *The War of the Flea: The Classic Study of Guerrilla Warfare* (Washington D.C.: Brassey's 2002), Kindle location 1190.
[25] Kenneth M. Pollack, *Arabs at War: Military Effectiveness, 1948-1991* (Lincoln: University of Nebraska Press 2002), Kindle location 2125.
[26] Ian Beckett and John Pimlott, *Counter-Insurgency: Lessons from History* (Barnsley: Pen and Sword 2011), Kindle Location 1900.
[27] Gary Klein, *Sources of Power: How People Make Decisions* (Cambridge: MIT Press 1999), pp. 31-33.
[28] Herbert Molloy Mason Jr., *The Rise of the Luftwaffe: 1918-1940* (New York: The Dial Press 1975), p. 349.
[29] Lind, Kindle Location 508.
[30] Linda Adams, "Learning a New Skill is Easier Said than Done," Gordon Training International, accessed at: http://www.gordontraining.com/free-workplace-articles/learning-a-new-skill-is-easier-said-than-done/#.
[31] LTC Dave Grossman, *On Combat: The Psychology and Physiology of Deadly Conflict in War and Peace* (Pensauken: BookBaby 2012), Kindle Location 1902.